ATOMIC ENERGY

History records that the Atomic Age commenced at 3:45 p.m., December 2, 1942, when a team of American scientists, working in wartime secrecy under the leadership of Enrico Fermi, achieved the first, self-sustaining nuclear fission reaction with an atomic 'pile' built beneath a stadium in the city of Chicago, Illinois.

Since World War II, our nation has been joined in the ability to make nuclear weapons by the Soviet Union, Great Britain, France and China. In recent years, most of the nuclear powers, recognizing the terrible threat a nuclear holocaust would pose to all mankind, have attempted to restrict the spread of nuclear weaponry and replace the world's burgeoning technology of war with one on peace—which would harness the atom's power for the benefit of the world.

This book is concerned with the peaceful uses of atomic energy in America and elsewhere, presenting a comprehensive picture of international progress on this broad front.

The author and editors wish to acknowledge indebtedness to the many institutions whose help proved invaluable in the preparation of this book: among them, in the United States, the Atomic Energy Commission, the Atomic Industrial Forum, and several corporations, including the General Electric Company; and in Great Britain, gratitude is owed, in particular, to the United Kingdom Atomic Energy Commission.

A
GROSSET
ALL-COLOR GUIDE

ATOMIC ENERGY

BY MATTHEW GAINES
Illustrated by Design Bureau

GROSSET & DUNLAP
A NATIONAL GENERAL COMPANY
Publishers • New York

191427

CONTENTS

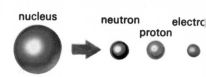

nucleus   neutron   electro
proton

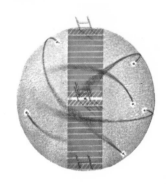

Electrostatic forces attract electrons to the protons in a nucleus.

A molecule of water contains two hydrogen atoms and an oxygen atom. The atoms are held together by electrostatic charge, like that given to a comb by passing it through the hair.

ATOMS

Everything is made up of atoms. They are about a hundredth of a millionth of an inch across, and there are many millions of them in a single breath of air. They were once thought to be hard, indivisible, spherical balls, but it is now known that they are made up of even smaller particles. Each atom has at its center a *nucleus,* consisting of *protons* and *neutrons.* Orbiting the nucleus are *electrons.* Every atom consists almost entirely of empty space, its size being indicated roughly by the orbit of its outermost electron. The nucleus and the electrons are each about a tenth of a millionth of a millionth of an inch across. Most of the mass of an atom is in the nucleus. Electrons are extremely light compared with protons and neutrons, which have nearly the same mass; the mass of the electron is only about $\frac{1}{1840}$ the mass of a proton, or neutron.

Electrons are negatively charged. They are held in the atom

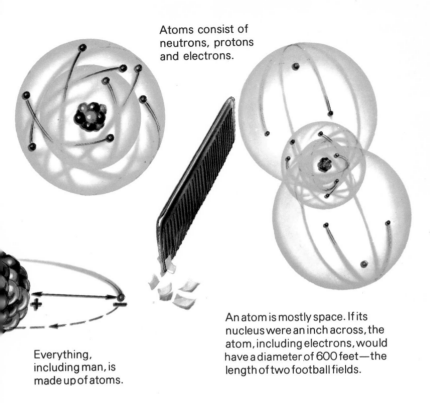

Atoms consist of neutrons, protons and electrons.

Everything, including man, is made up of atoms.

An atom is mostly space. If its nucleus were an inch across, the atom, including electrons, would have a diameter of 600 feet—the length of two football fields.

by the equal, positive charge of the protons in the nucleus. Neutrons have no electric charge. Because the atom is electrically neutral, the number of orbital electrons it has must equal the number of protons in the nucleus. This number is important because it 'identifies' a chemical element; it is called the *atomic number,* sometimes represented by the symbol Z.

The orbits of the electrons are arranged in *shells,* which scientists label *K, L, M, N,* and so on, moving from the innermost orbit outward. The *K* layer contains 2 orbits, the *L* layer 8, the *M* layer 18, the *N* layer 32, with only one electron in each orbit. The lowest-energy orbits are the inner ones, and these are the most stable. In atoms with a low atomic number—that is, with few electrons—only the innermost orbits are filled.

Ninety kinds of atoms, with varying chemical properties, occur naturally on the earth. They are the chemical elements, such as hydrogen, oxygen, carbon, gold and uranium.

Nuclei

The number of protons and neutrons in the nucleus increases as we move from the simplest atom to the most complex. The simplest atom is hydrogen, with one proton as its nucleus and one orbital electron; the atomic number (Z) is 1, and the number of neutrons (N) is 0. This is the commonest form of hydrogen; a rare form, called deuterium or heavy hydrogen, has a neutron in addition to the proton, and an even rarer form, tritium, has two neutrons. These three forms of hydrogen, chemically identical, have mass numbers $(A = Z + N)$ of 1, 2, and 3, respectively. The atom with a mass of 4 has two neutrons like tritium, but two protons and two orbital electrons; this is helium, and its chemical properties are very different from those of hydrogen, deuterium or tritium atoms.

mass number (= Z + N) A X symbol protons Z N neutrons		Protons	Neutrons	Electrons	
HYDROGEN	$^1_1H_0$	●	none	●	
DEUTERIUM	$^2_1H_1$	●	●	●	Chemically identical
TRITIUM	$^3_1H_2$	●	● ●	●	
HELIUM	$^4_2He_2$	● ●	● ●	● ●	

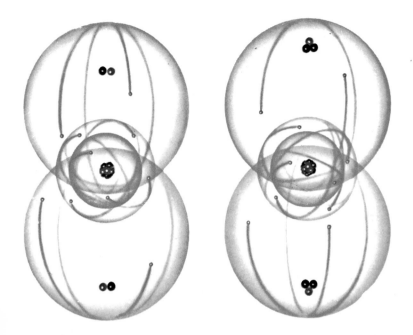

Molecules of heavy water or deuterium oxide, D_2O (*left*), and tritium oxide, T_2O (*right*). The chemical properties of these substances are like those of water, H_2O, but the physical properties differ.

The term used to describe a nucleus, with reference to its number of protons and neutrons, is *nuclide*. When a group of nuclides have equal numbers of protons (i.e., the same atomic number) but different numbers of neutrons, they are called *isotopes*. The three hydrogen nuclides, for example, are commonly referred to as the three isotopes of hydrogen. Chemical elements usually exist naturally as a mixture of isotopes, but in atomic energy it is necessary to consider one nuclide at a time. A nuclide is identified by the formula $^A_Z X_N$, X being the chemical symbol. The cobalt nuclide, containing 27 protons and 33 neutrons, is written $^{60}_{27}Co_{33}$. Often an abbreviated form is used: $_{27}Co^{60}$, ^{60}Co, Co^{60}, or cobalt-60. A chart of the known nuclides, including those that are man-made is given on pages 8 and 9. The nuclei of the isotopes colored pink are *radioactive*—they contain an unstable arrangement of protons and neutrons and *disintegrate* spontaneously, emitting *radiation*.

Chart of the Nuclides

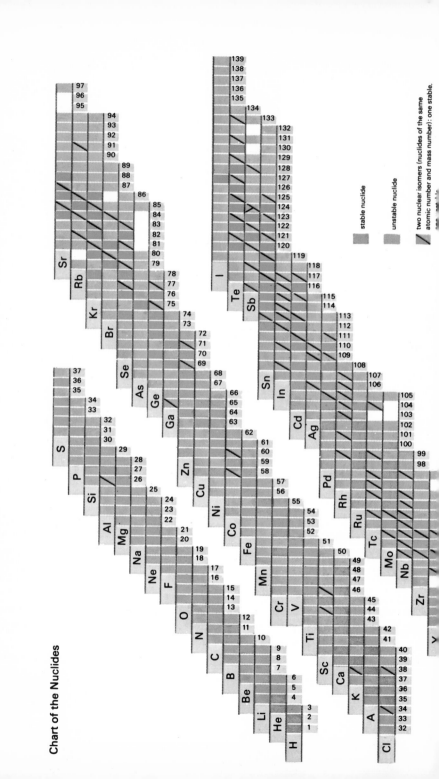

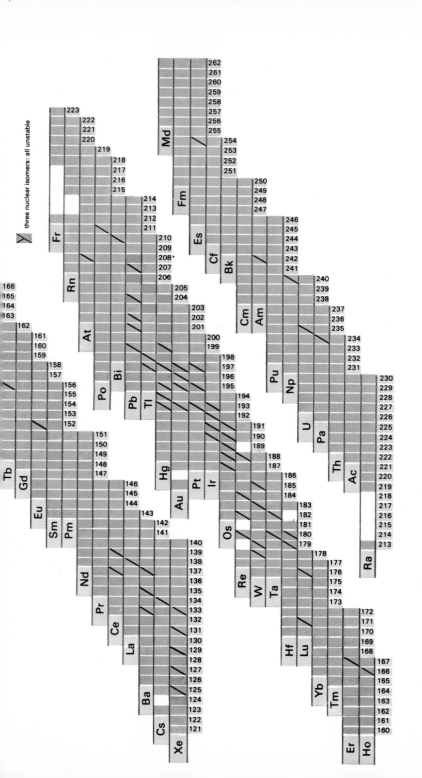

three nuclear isomers: all unstable

Alpha particles are stopped by paper.

Beta particles are stopped by thin sheets of metal.

Gamma rays penetrate several inches of metal.

Radioactivity

Radioactivity was discovered in 1896 by the French scientist Henri Becquerel, who found that pitchblende ore—which contains uranium—fogged photographic plates, even when they were wrapped in black paper. Clearly some sort of penetrating radiation was involved. It is now known that this radiation consisted of alpha (α) particles. Radioactive materials can emit two other types of radiation also: beta (β) and gamma (γ). Alpha particles are not very penetrating. They are stopped by a few sheets of paper or a few inches of air. Beta particles are more penetrating than alpha particles, but they are stopped by thick cardboard, thin sheets of metal such as aluminium, or a few feet of air. Gamma rays are radiations similar to X-rays, and are very penetrating indeed. It may take several inches of metal to reduce gamma radiation to a harmless level.

An Alpha particle is a helium-4 nucleus consisting of two protons and two neutrons. It has a positive charge of two and a mass number of four. Therefore, the nuclide emitting an alpha

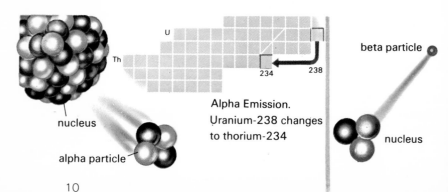

nucleus

alpha particle

Alpha Emission. Uranium-238 changes to thorium-234

beta particle

nucleus

particle obviously deteriorates into another nuclide with an atomc number two units less and a mass number four units less. For instance, the alpha disintegration of uranium-238 gives thorium-234. This reaction is represented as follows:

$$_{92}U^{238} \longrightarrow \ _2He^4 + \ _{90}Th^{234} \quad \text{or} \quad U^{238} \xrightarrow{\ a\ } Th^{234}$$

Beta particles are also emitted by the nucleus. There are two types of beta particles: electrons and positrons (positive electrons). The type emitted depends upon the kind of nuclear deterioration that occurs.

A negative electron, β^-, is produced when a neutron changes into a proton. The nuclide in which this occurs is transformed into one of the same mass number but with an atomic number higher by one. For instance, tritium, $_1H^3$ emits negative electrons from its nucleus, becoming an isotope of helium, $_2He^3$. This reaction is represented as follows:

$$_1H^3 \longrightarrow \beta^- + \ _2He^3 \quad \text{or} \quad H^3 \xrightarrow{\ \beta^-\ } He^3$$

A positron, β^+, is emitted by a proton changing into a neutron. Again, a nuclide with the same mass number is produced—this time with an atomic number lower by one. For instance, the phosphorus isotope $_{15}P^{30}$ emits a positron and turns into a silicon isotope $_{14}Si^{30}$. This reaction is written as follows:

$$_{15}P^{30} \longrightarrow \beta^+ + \ _{14}Si^{30} \quad \text{or} \quad P^{30} \xrightarrow{\ \beta^+\ } Si^{30}$$

In a few cases, both positrons and electrons are emitted from a nucleus. For instance, the nuclide $_{29}Cu^{64}$ lies between the

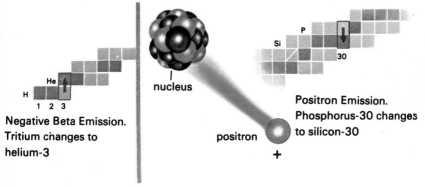

Negative Beta Emission. Tritium changes to helium-3

nucleus

positron

Positron Emission. Phosphorus-30 changes to silicon-30

11

two stable copper nuclides $_{29}Cu^{63}$ and $_{29}Cu^{65}$ and decays thus:

$$_{29}Cu^{64} \rightarrow \beta^+ + {}_{28}Ni^{64} \quad and \quad {}_{29}Cu^{64} \rightarrow \beta^- + {}_{30}Zn^{64}$$

It should be noted that copper-63 and copper-65 are not produced, because it is the atomic numbers of the product that change through beta radiation, not the mass numbers.

If the energy needed to break up the nucleus is greater than the binding energy of the neutron in the compound nucleus, then the nucleus can be fissioned only by neutrons possessing this extra energy—that is, *fast neutrons*. Fission of uranium-238, for instance, requires neutrons moving with energies of not less than 1•1 MeV. Neutrons with energies of less than this produce an excited uranium-239 nucleus, which decays to give the important fissile nuclide plutonium-239. Because it can so easily be converted to a fissile nuclide, uranium-238 is said to be *fertile*.

As the basic requirement for fission is energy sufficient to shatter the nucleus, methods other than neutron-capture can also be used to achieve the splitting of an atom. Fission has been obtained with high-energy alpha particles, deuterons and protons. However, none of these reactions is of practical value, as they require the expenditure of large amounts of energy to enable the charged particles to penetrate the fissile nuclei. Neutrons, on the other hand, are uncharged and can thus penetrate nuclei much more easily. Consequently, neutron-induced fission is the basic reaction that produces both the explosions of some atomic weapons and the heat of nuclear reactors.

When a radioactive nuclide (or *radionuclide*) has ejected an alpha or beta particle, its nucleus has excess energy. It loses this energy by emitting *gamma rays*. For example, in the reaction

$$_{27}Co^{60} \rightarrow \beta^+ + {}_{26}Ni^{60}$$

the Ni nuclide is produced in an *excited state,* and emits gamma rays in reaching its *ground state* (the normal state of minimum energy).

The most convenient way of describing the rate at which a radioactive material loses its radioactivity is in terms of its *half-*

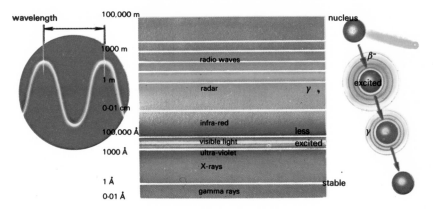

wavelength

100,000 m
1000 m
radio waves
1 m
radar γ
0·01 cm
infra-red
100,000 Å less
visible light excited
1000 Å
ultra-violet
X-rays
1 Å
gamma rays
0·01 Å

nucleus
β⁻
excited
γ
stable

Every radiation has a certain wavelength, the distance between peaks of energy in the wave produced (*left*). Gamma rays are electromagnetic radiation with a very short wavelength (*center*). This radiation is emitted by excited nuclei (*right*).

life. This is the time in which half the number of radioactive atoms in a substance will decay. Half-lives vary from small fractions of a second to millions of years, depending upon the nuclides concerned. Half-lives are constant. They are not affected by the physical or chemical condition of a radioactive material, or by its age.

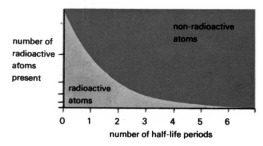

number of radioactive atoms present

non-radioactive atoms

radioactive atoms

0 1 2 3 4 5 6
number of half-life periods

After the first half-life period, half the original number of radioactive atoms remain. After the second, a quarter remain, and so on.

Nuclide Masses

The masses of atomic particles are extremely small, but they have been determined with great accuracy. The unit of measurement is the Atomic Mass Unit (amu), which is defined as $\frac{1}{16}$ the mass of the oxygen nuclide $^{16}_{8}O$. The mass of the neutron is 1.008982 amu, and that of the proton 1.007593 amu. But the *deuteron* (the nucleus of the deuterium atom), consisting

13

of a neutron and proton, weighs only 2.014194 amu, an apparent loss in mass of 0.002381 amu. This loss is called the *mass defect*.

When a proton and neutron form a deuteron, a certain amount of energy is released. Conversely, the same amount of energy must be supplied to the deuteron to break it apart. It is this energy that accounts for the mass defect. All nuclei undergo energy changes when they are formed, and all have a mass defect. As with the deuteron, the defect corresponds to the energy needed to break the nucleus into its component parts, or *nucleons*. This energy is called the *binding energy*.

Binding Energy

The greater the binding energy of a nucleus, the greater is its stability. To calculate binding energy, Einstein's mass-energy relation, $E = mc^2$, is used. Here, E is the energy corresponding to a definite mass m, and c (a constant) is the velocity of light in a vacuum (3×10^{10} cm/sec). By substituting the mass defect for m in the Einstein equation, E, the binding energy, is calculated. It is expressed in MeV (millions of *electron-volts*), the unit of energy used in nuclear physics. The mass defect of the helium-4 nucleus, for example, is 0.030374 amu, and the binding energy is about 28 MeV.

The mass converted into energy in the formation of a deuteron makes it lighter than its detached neutron and proton.

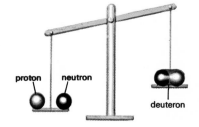

proton   neutron

deuteron

Scientists rarely use total binding energy in their calculations, but refer instead to the average energy released by each nucleon (neutron or proton) in the formation of a nucleus. Called the *binding energy per nucleon*, this quality is obtained simply by dividing the binding energy by the number of nucleons. Binding energy per nucleon is not the same for every nuclide. In fact, it varies in a regular fashion with the mass numbers of the nuclides. The binding energies per nucleon of light nuclei show a rising trend to a peak value of about 8.7 MeV for nuclides with about 50 or 60 nucleons (e.g., iron, nickel), and then gradually drop off to about 7.5 MeV for uranium-238.

The curve helps to explain why there are two ways in which energy can be released from atomic nuclei. Because nuclei are more stable the greater their binding energy per nucleon, any reaction in which nuclei in lower parts of the curve area rearranged to form nuclei higher up the curve will release energy. The first class of reactions that do this involves the *fusion* (adding together) of light nuclei, and the second involves the *fission* (splitting) of heavy nuclei. The fission of uranium-235 has been harnessed in nuclear reactors, mainly to produce electricity, and this reaction will be looked at more closely now. The fusion of light nuclei will be described in the chapter on Thermonuclear Fusion.

The binding energy per nucleon is the average amount of energy needed to detach a neutron or proton from a nucleus. It is highest for elements with mass numbers between 50 and 60.

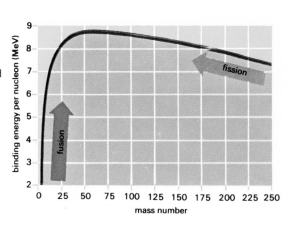

Fission

When a uranium-235 nucleus is struck by a neutron, fission takes place: the nucleus splits into two nuclei of medium atomic weight and releases a vast amount of energy — about 190 MeV. But fission would never have acquired its importance as a source of energy if it were not for the fact that when the nucleus splits it also ejects two or three neutrons. These neutrons can penetrate more nuclei, causing further fissions and re-

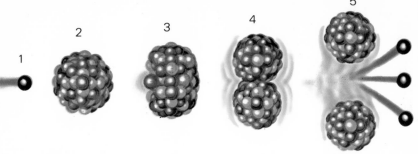

When a neutron (1) and a uranium nucleus (2) collide (3), the uranium nucleus becomes unstable (4). It splits into two smaller nuclei, releasing neutrons and energy to regain stability (5). This process is called fission.

leasing more energy and more neutrons. They produce, in fact, a self-sustaining chain reaction. The nuclei produced are called *fission products*. They fly apart at terrific velocities, colliding with other nuclei, causing the random motion of all the atoms in the material to increase — in other words, make the material heat up. Since the fission process takes less than a millionth of a second, enormous outputs of energy can quickly be achieved. If all the atoms in one pound of uranium-235 were fissioned, the energy released would be equivalent to that from burning 3,000,000 tons of coal.

When a nucleus captures a neutron, an *excited* compound nucleus is initially produced. It has an *excitation energy* equal to the neutron binding energy in the compound nucleus plus the kinetic energy of the neutron prior to capture. If the excitation energy is high enough, the nucleus will vibrate until it splits; this is called the *fission process*. If, however, it is insufficient to cause fission, the nucleus loses its excess energy by radioactive decay.

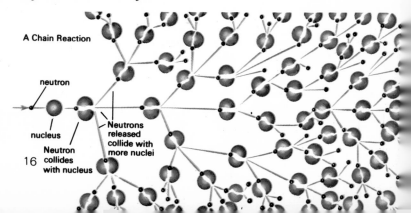

A Chain Reaction

neutron

nucleus

Neutron collides with nucleus

Neutrons released collide with more nuclei

16

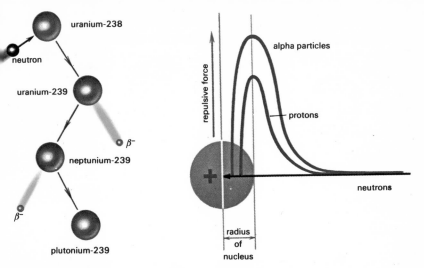

Slow neutrons cause uranium-238 to produce fissile plutonium-239 (*left*). Charged particles such as protons and alpha particles experience repulsive forces as they approach the charged nucleus that are not experienced by the neutron (*right*).

Whether a nucleus will fission depends upon whether the energy needed to break it up is greater than or less than the binding energy of the neutron in the excited compound nucleus. If it is lower than the neutron binding energy, the nucleus can be fissioned by a *slow neutron*, one with negligible kinetic energy. Of all the naturally occurring nuclides, only uranium-235 is fissioned by slow neutrons. However, some artificial nuclides, notably plutonium-239 and uranium-233, can also be fissioned by slow neutrons. Such nuclides are said to be *fissile*.

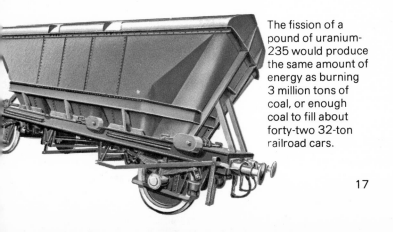

The fission of a pound of uranium-235 would produce the same amount of energy as burning 3 million tons of coal, or enough coal to fill about forty-two 32-ton railroad cars.

17

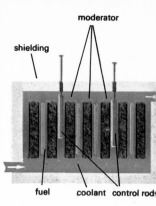

The first nuclear reactor achieved a self-sustaining chain reaction on December 2, 1942 at the University of Chicago.

The basic components of a nuclear reactor shown in diagrammatic form

REACTORS

Nuclear reactors have the following basic components: fuel, control system, coolant, shielding, and, in most cases, a *moderator*.

A neutron freshly produced in a fission reaction travels at 10,000 miles a second. If it hits a uranium-235 atom it causes fission. But since in natural uranium there is only one U-235 atom for every 140 U-238 atoms, there is not much chance of a fast neutron hitting a uranium-235 atom and producing another fission. In fact, a neutron is more likely to do this if it travels at about 1 mile a second.

There are, therefore, two ways of making a reactor: either the fast neutrons are slowed or the proportion of fissile atoms is greatly increased. A moderator slows down neutrons, without absorbing them. Good moderators are light atoms such as hydrogen (in water), deuterium (in heavy water), and carbon (in graphite). The slow neutrons are called *thermal* neutrons; hence reactors that use moderators are called thermal reactors.

Reactors relying on fast neutrons to maintain the chain reaction are called *fast* reactors. They use fuel in which the propor-

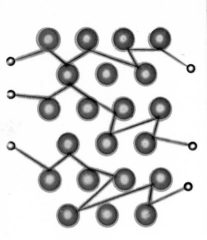

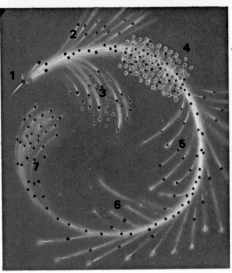

A moderator slows neutrons without abosrbing them (*left*), but few of the neutrons involved in fission actually cause fission (*right*). Of the neutrons produced by initial fissions (1), fast neutrons escape (2) or are absorbed in uranium-238 (3); the moderator slows remaining fast neutrons (4) but many of these escape (5) or are absorbed (6) before further fissions occur (7).

tion of fissile material has been considerably enriched by the addition of either plutonium-239 or more uranium-235.

In both thermal and fast reactors the 'population' of neutrons, which maintain the chain reaction, is controlled with powerful neutron-absorbing materials such as cadmium, hafnium, and boron, usually in the form of rods. These rods, lowered into the reactor, absorb neutrons, slow down the reaction, and reduce the reactor output. Raising the rods allows the reaction to build up again. The positioning of the control rods in the reactor gives a steady reaction rate.

Most of the energy released by fission is in the form of heat. Normally, to put this heat to use, a coolant is passed through the reactor core, transferring the heat to a boiler to produce steam. Immense quantities of heat are generated in reactors used to produce electricity or propel submarines; as a result, the cooling system must be efficient to avoid overheating and melting of the reactor core. The coolant must be cheap and non-

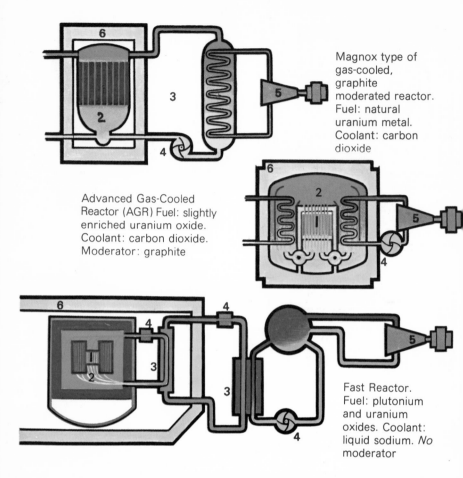

Magnox type of gas-cooled, graphite moderated reactor. Fuel: natural uranium metal. Coolant: carbon dioxide

Advanced Gas-Cooled Reactor (AGR) Fuel: slightly enriched uranium oxide. Coolant: carbon dioxide. Moderator: graphite

Fast Reactor. Fuel: plutonium and uranium oxides. Coolant: liquid sodium. *No* moderator

corrosive, and must not absorb neutrons. Coolants used include gases such as carbon dioxide and helium, liquids such as ordinary water, heavy water, and fluid organic compounds, and liquid metals such as sodium. Sometimes the functions of coolant and moderator are combined in a single material, such as ordinary water.

Shielding is necessary to protect the public and reactor operators from neutrons and gamma radiation given off by the fission products. Quite often the shielding consists of concrete many feet thick, frequently with a steel inner shield to reduce the speed of fast neutrons before they enter the concrete.

In building a reactor a vital requirement is to have a *critical*

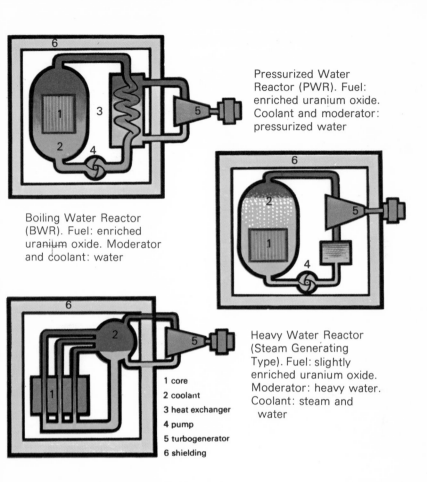

Pressurized Water Reactor (PWR). Fuel: enriched uranium oxide. Coolant and moderator: pressurized water

Boiling Water Reactor (BWR). Fuel: enriched uranium oxide. Moderator and coolant: water

Heavy Water Reactor (Steam Generating Type). Fuel: slightly enriched uranium oxide. Moderator: heavy water. Coolant: steam and water

1 core
2 coolant
3 heat exchanger
4 pump
5 turbogenerator
6 shielding

mass of fuel—that is, sufficient fissile material in an arrangement that will maintain a chain reaction. If the mass is too small or arranged in the wrong shape, too many neutrons will escape and the chain reaction will peter out. Another factor to be taken into account is the absorption of neutrons by structural materials, by the coolant, and by non-fissile materials in the fuel. When the chain reaction is self-sustaining, *criticality* is said to have been reached. An artificial supply of neutrons is usually necessary to start a chain reaction.

The basic arrangement of fuel, moderator, coolant, and shielding in the six most important types of reactor is shown on these two pages.

Magnox Reactors

The world's first industrial nuclear power station employed gas-cooled reactors. Situated at Calder Hall, in Cumberland, England, it opened in October 1956. Its four reactors were the forerunners of a series of gas-cooled reactors built in Britian and elsewhere to produce electricity. The output of Calder Hall is 180 MW(e) (megawatts* of electricity). But this type of reactor underwent successive development with each station built, and 1180 MW(e) will be produced from the twin reactor plant under construction at Wylfa Point, Anglesey.

In all such reactors the fuel is natural uranium. The uranium metal is in the form of rods encased in a magnesium alloy called *magnox*—hence this name is used to describe such reactors. The magnox container is finned to provide good heat transfer between the reactor and the coolant gas.

The graphite moderator is arranged in the form of a square lattice of bricks with vertical channels. The fuel elements are stacked in these channels, with some of the channels occupied by control rods made of boron steel. The coolant—carbon

*1 megawatt = 1000 kilowatts

Calder Hall in Great Britain, the world's first nuclear power station

dioxide gas—flows up through the channels and over the fuel elements. In Britain's Hinkley Point 'A' station shown below there are 36,000 fuel elements in 500 channels, making 376 metric tons* of uranium in all. Coolant flows through the core at the rate of about 5 tons per second.

The core of a gas-cooled reactor is surrounded by a graphite reflector that bounces back some of the escaping neutrons.

The coolant carrying the heat from the reactor (at between 350° and 400°C) is used to boil water to produce steam for the turbogenerator. The gas leaving the heat exchanger is returned to the reactor by large powerful blowers. A concrete shield around the reactor gives protection to operators and the public. The heat exchanger need not be provided with a biological shield; although the carbon dioxide gas passes right through the reactor core, it does not become radioactive.

Most of these gas-cooled plants have complex devices above the reactor to refuel it while it is operating.

*1 metric ton = 2201.6 lb.

Hinkley Point 'A' nuclear power station, Great Britain

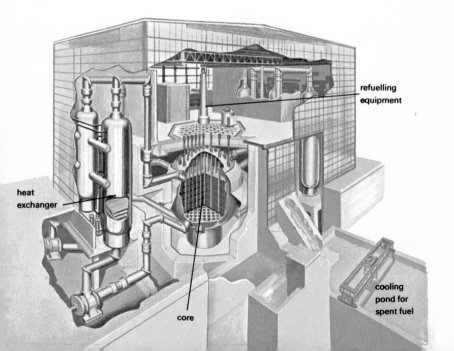

refuelling equipment

heat exchanger

cooling pond for spent fuel

core

Advanced Gas-cooled Reactors (AGR)

Although the magnox stations represented a continuous development of gas-cooled reactors, to improve the system still further and to reduce capital and generating costs it was necessary to increase the operating temperature so as to increase thermal efficiency and to extract more heat from the fuel. The main difference in these so-called *advanced gas-cooled reactors* is that they use as fuel ceramic uranium dioxide canned in stainless steel. Because the stainless steel absorbs neutrons, and also because the fuel is in the form of an oxide, the uranium-235content of the fuel must be increased slightly. However, the coolant and moderator are the same as in the magnox stations and, although AGRs are considerably more compact, much of the design, construction, and mode of operation is the same.

The first AGR was built at Windscale, England, a site adjacent to Calder Hall. It was commissioned in 1962 and now has a capacity of 33 MW(e). Its main purpose, however, was to prove that this system, and particularly the fuel, would work satisfactorily.

The good performance of this reactor and the improvement

Windscale advanced gas-cooled reactor, Great Britain

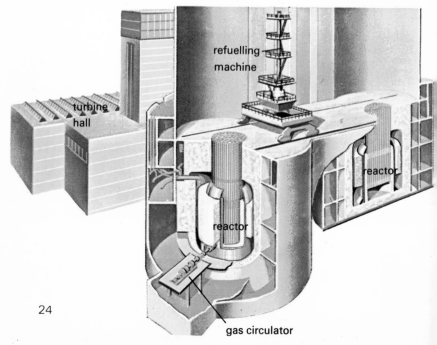

of the graphite needed for commercial versions helped to establish AGRs as successors to magnox reactors in the British nuclear power program. However, the AGR was accepted (in 1965) only after a detailed comparison with American boiling water reactors (BWR) and pressurized water reactors (PWR) in the assessment of tenders for the second station at Dungeness, England. It was shown that AGRs would generate electricity some 10 percent more cheaply than the best water-cooled reactor (a BWR) and over 10 percent more cheaply than the most modern coal-fired station then coming into service. A particular advantage of the AGR was shown to be the system of on-load refueling, together with fuel in the form of graphite sleeves, each containing 36 stainless-steel-clad uranium oxide rods. With the temperatures obtained in the AGR (the coolant will leave the Dungeness 'B' reactors at 402° C) the thermal efficiency is 41 percent—far higher than that in coal-fired stations.

Gas-cooled reactors have also been developed in France. Although the French nuclear power program has not been on the same scale as the British it has shown some interesting innovations—the French were the first to use pre-stressed concrete pressure vessels. The French are also building other kinds of thermal reactors.

Dungeness 'B' nuclear power station, Great Britain

Pressurized Water Reactors (PWR)

The coolant in these reactors is ordinary water under very high pressure. It is heated to about 580° C, the high pressure preventing it from boiling, and passes to a heat exchanger where it boils water flowing in a secondary circuit, to produce steam. The pressurized water also acts as the moderator.

The fuel in a modern PWR is enriched uranium oxide pellets, large numbers of which are fitted into zirconium tubes to form rods running the length of the reactor core. Zirconium is used because it is resistant to corrosion by hot water. The rods are arranged in groups of fuel assemblies, and the gaps between them must be kept small because water is a very powerful moderator.

Owing to the high pressure of the coolant, the pressure vessel must be made of very thick steel. However, a PWR is a very compact reactor, smaller than a boiling water reactor or gas-cooled reactor of equivalent power. It is, of course, housed in a biological shield, as are the heat exchangers, because the water from the core is radioactive.

U.S.S. *Nautilus,* the first nuclear powered submarine

An interesting aspect of PWRs is the use of 'chemical shim'. This is a way of compensating for long-term reactivity changes associated with fuel depletion and fission product build-up mixing a soluble neutron absorber (boron as boric acid) with the coolant. But control rods are still used. They are clusters of silver-indium-cadmium alloy rods moving in the fuel assemblies in spaces where fuel rods have been omitted. Their purpose, apart from reactor shut-down, is to change the reactor power level to match the demand on the reactor. But chemical shim takes care of long-term variations in reactivity, and only a relatively small number of rods is needed—60 in a 1000 MW (e) plant compared with 150 if chemical shim were not used. During each refueling shut-down, only one-third of the fuel assemblies are replaced and the fuel is rearranged to obtain the best power distribution for the next cycle.

A PWR powered the U.S.S. *Nautilus,* the first nuclear submarine, which began trials in 1955. In 1957 an experimental power station using a PWR was commissioned at Shippingport, Pennsylvania. Many others have followed.

Reactor core of power plant at Shippingport, Pennsylvania

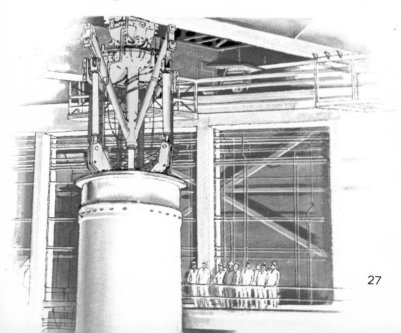

Boiling Water Reactors (BWR)

Water is also the coolant and moderator in boiling water reactors, but it is not pressurized; it is allowed to boil in the reactor. A BWR is therefore like a 'nuclear kettle', with fuel (enriched uranium oxide in zirconium alloy) instead of a heating element. The steam passes from the top of the reactor direct to the turbogenerator.

A BWR is a relatively simple reactor. It has no heat exchanger, and the reactor pressure vessel has to withstand much smaller pressures than that in a PWR and, therefore, has thinner walls.

However, the modern BWR has evolved through a series of designs intended to overcome a problem inherent in this type of reactor. As the water boils in the core, bubbles form that change the moderating and neutron-absorbing properties of the coolant/moderator, and also affect the transfer of heat from the fuel. To cope with this, the main body of the water is pumped out from the core and returned at a lower point.

It was a direct-cycle BWR that achieved the 'economic breakthrough' in electricity generation in the United States. It has been established that the station, a 515 MW(e) plant at Oyster Creek, New Jersey, generates electricity more cheaply than a coal station would in that area. This reaction has served

Dresden nuclear power station in Illinois.

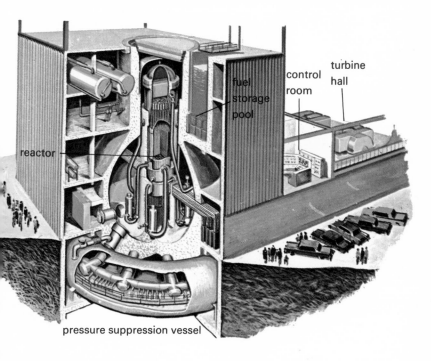

reactor

fuel
storage
pool

control
room

turbine
hall

pressure suppression vessel

Oyster Creek, New Jersey nuclear power station, the first in
America to compete with coal

as the prototype for a large number of other BWRs in the
United States and abroad. The size of many of these have been
greater than that at Oyster Creek, up to about 1000 MW(e).
The Oyster Creek plant also introduced a new safety feature,
'pressure suppression'. With this system, any steam escaping
from the reactor would be condensed in cool water, instead of
being given a large volume of space in which to expand.

Acceptance of the BWR was delayed initially because of
doubts about its safety, but these were resolved by a spectacu-
lar series of experiments. The doubts had arisen because the
effect of the formation of bubbles in a reactor core was appar-
ently unpredictable. But it turned out that, even when the
reactor was given enough reactivity to blow out some of the
core, the bubbles formed quickly enough to stop the reaction
before the components left the reactor.

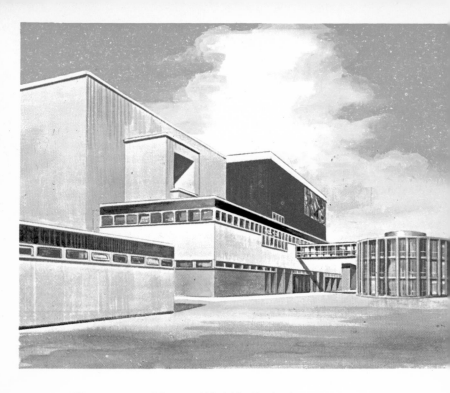

The reactor buildings at Winfrith, England.

Heavy Water Reactors

Heavy water is a better moderator than light water because it absorbs far fewer neutrons and allows them to travel much farther before they slow down to the level of thermal energies. Consequently, fuel elements can be inches apart instead of a tenth of an inch as in light water reactors, and the core is less crowded.

Basically, there are two ways of constructing heavy water reactors: one using a pressure vessel, the other pressure tubes. In the latter the heavy water moderator is separated from the coolant in a *calandria*, a large tank with tubes through it. The pressure tubes, which are inserted in the calandria tubes, contain the fuel; and the coolant, which may be heavy water, light water, gas or steam, passes through the pressure tubes.

Canada has concentrated on heavy water reactors and the established 'Candu' reactor is of pressure-tube construction with heavy water as moderator and pressurized heavy water as coolant; the coolant is used to boil light water in a heat exchanger. The reactor is controlled by the level of the moderator in the calandria.

In Britain, a 100 MW(e) heavy water reactor has been built at Winfrith, in Dorset. Called the steam generating heavy water reactor (SGHWR), it uses light water as coolant, boiling it in the pressure tubes and feeding some of it directly to the turbine. The rest is returned to superheat channels in the reactor core and heated to 504° C before passing to the turbine.

Heavy water reactors cooled by carbon dioxide have been built in France (the 73 MW(e) EL-4 at Brennils), Czechoslovakia (the 150 MW(e) reactor at Bohunice), and Germany (the 150 MW(e) KKN reactor at Niederaichbach).

Heavy water reactors using pressure vessels have been built in Sweden. At Marviken a 194 MW(e) boiling heavy water reactor has been built which feeds heavy water steam direct to the turbine. It will eventually be made to superheat some of the steam. A pressurized heavy water reactor has been built at Agesta to provide power and heating for the Farsta suburb of Stockholm.

Lowering the calandria into place in Britain's Winfrith steam generating heavy water reactor

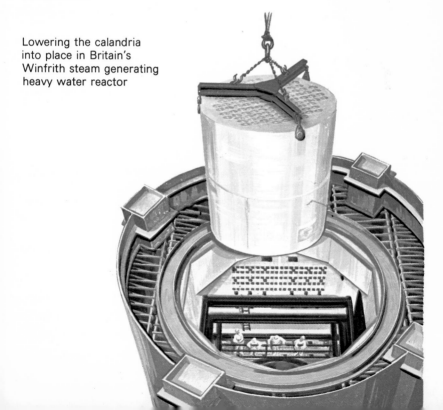

Other Types of Thermal Reactors

In addition to the established reactors previously described there are others that could become economically important in future years. High-temperature reactors (HTR) are gas-cooled thermal reactors having small cores with high power density (the rate at which heat is released per unit volume of core is high). They also enable conversion of fertile material (e.g., thorium) to fissile material.

The first HTR to be built was the 'Dragon' reactor, a small experimental reactor at Winfrith, in Dorset, England. The coolant is helium, which leaves the core at a temperature of

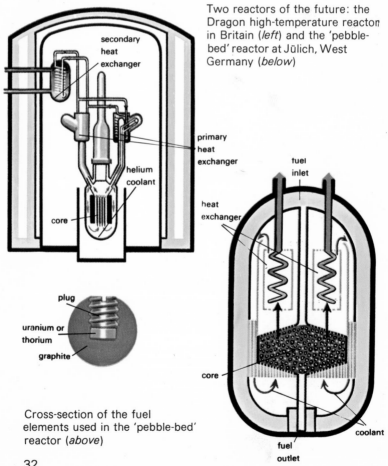

Two reactors of the future: the Dragon high-temperature reactor in Britain (*left*) and the 'pebble-bed' reactor at Jülich, West Germany (*below*)

secondary heat exchanger

primary heat exchanger

helium coolant

core

plug

uranium or thorium

graphite

heat exchanger

fuel inlet

core

coolant

fuel outlet

Cross-section of the fuel elements used in the 'pebble-bed' reactor (*above*)

Obinsk, an early Russian water-cooled graphite-moderated plant

Piqua, Ohio, cooled and moderated by organic compounds

750° C. The purpose of the Dragon reactor is to demonstrate the principles on which a high-temperature, gas-cooled power reactor could be built. The reactor reached full power in 1965. Another HTR, the AVR or pebble-bed reactor, has been built at Julich Nuclear Research Estabishment in North Rhine-Westphalia, West Germany. This reactor also is cooled by helium gas, but the core is homogeneous and highly enriched, using fuel elements in the form of 6 cm. graphite spheres. They are poured slowly through the core while the reactor is operating.

It has been suggested that HTRs could be built in which the hot gas passes from the core directly to a gas-turbine, thus eliminating heat exchangers. Russia has built several graphite/water reactors, which have a graphite moderator, uranium metal fuel (enriched 5 percent), and are cooled by pressurized water that produces steam in a heat exchanger. In the United States, large graphite/water reactors are used for plutonium production at Richland, Washington.

Another thermal reactor is the organic moderated and cooled type. At Piqua, Ohio, a small reactor moderated and cooled by a commercial mixture of organic compounds has been operated. A related type of reactor is organically moderated, while cooled by heavy water.

33

Dounreay fast reactor, Scotland.

Fast Reactors

In a fast reactor, the absence of a moderator means that the neutrons do not slow down very much. It also means that the core is very small and the fuel considerably enriched in fissile atoms, either with more uranium-235 or with plutonium-239. In addition, fast reactors are designed with a very small proportion of absorbents in the core in the form of structural materials, coolant, etc. The net result is that very few neutrons are wasted.

This 'neutron economy' is further improved by placing around the core a blanket of uranium-238. Any neutrons escaping from the core are thus absorbed, and plutonium-239 is eventually produced by the decay process shown on page 17. Unabsorbed neutrons are reflected into the core.

Thus, as the reactor burns up its original load of fuel it also 'breeds' new fuel from the uranium-238 blanket and the U-238 in the core. This new fuel can be separated chemically and used in other fast reactors. Some of the uranium-238 in thermal reactors is also converted to plutonium-239. The most economical use of this is in fast reactors.

Although fast reactors are small in size they produce vast quantities of heat. The problem for the designer is to find materials that can stand up to this intense heat, and in particular to find a suitable coolant to transfer the heat from the core. In several nations liquid sodium is being used.

Sodium melts at 98° C and boils at 880° C. It conducts heat well and has good nuclear properties. But using it has necessitated the development of a new technology, in the form of components for coolant circuits—including pumps, pipes, heat exchangers and instruments.

For example, one of the problems that arises with sodium is keeping it pure. It dissolves oxygen from the walls of the pipes to form sodium oxide. This is soluble at high temperatures but tends to crystallize on the cooler parts of the circuit and eventually causes blockage. Impurities also tend to increase the rate of corrosion of pipe walls. Cold traps have therefore been devel-

Impression of the 250 MW (e) prototype reactor at Dounreay, Scotland.

Rapsodie, built by France in cooperation with Euratom

oped. Such traps are designed so that the impurities are precipitated in them, without causing blockage.

Mechanical pumps have been developed for the large volume flow needed in the big fast reactors. The innovations in these pumps include a bearing that operates submerged in sodium and is lubricated by the sodium itself.

Because the heat rating in a fast reactor is high, the fuel burns quickly. In fact, in a fast reactor there are as many fissions in a month as there are in several years in a thermal reactor. In metallic fuels the irradiation damage would be severe, and they would have to be removed from the reactor after a short time. Fuels have therefore been developed which are better able to withstand the changes caused by the fission products. They are ceramic mixtures of uranium and plutonium oxides. The successful development of these new fuels has been a key element in the fast reactor program in Britain.

Development of fast reactors is now the most important single project of the United Kingdom Atomic Energy Authority. Having designed and built the 14 MW(e) experimental fast reactor at Dounreay and having obtained experience in using this sodium-cooled reactor to generate electricity and test fuels, the UKAEA is now building a 250 MW(e) prototype fast reactor (PFR), also at Dounreay. This will be completed in 1970 and will generate power in 1971. The PFR will demonstrate the operating characteristics of large stations—of 1000 MW(e) or more. It will also 'prove' the fast-reactor technology, by showing whether the fuel elements and other components can be adapted to the commercial versions.

A prototype of similar size will be completed at the same time in Russia at Shevchenko. The reactor core will use enriched uranium changing over to its own plutonium as this becomes available.

The United States has scored a success with its Experimental Breeder Reactor 11 (similar in size to the Dounreay fast reactor). As yet, however, the performance of the 100 MW(e) Enrico Fermi reactor remains disappointing. France has built an experimental fast reactor, 'Rapsodie', at Cadarache, and plans a 250 MW(e) prototype, 'Phenix'. Germany is investigating steam-cooled fast reactors, and intends to build a 300 MW(e) prototype. But the Germans are also interested in sodium cooling, and plan another 300 MW(e) prototype utilizing this system. Small experimental reactors using these coolants have been built, the 25 MW(e) steam-cooled Grosswelzheim (HDR) and the 20 MW(e) Karlsruhe (KNK).

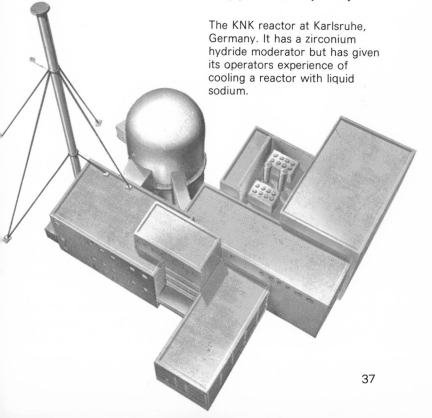

The KNK reactor at Karlsruhe, Germany. It has a zirconium hydride moderator but has given its operators experience of cooling a reactor with liquid sodium.

Research Reactors

A research reactor is designed to provide a source of neutrons and gamma rays. The widespread existence of such reactors—over 300 are in operation throughout the world—has arisen because of the usefulness of neutrons and gamma radiation in a variety of scientific investigations, apart from their interest to nuclear physicists. For example, scientists can learn the structure of materials by observing the way in which they scatter streams of neutrons. Chemists analyze unknown substances by first irradiating them in a reactor, then examining the radiation given off by the material—a clue to the identity of the sample. The effects of radiation on many materials can be discovered by irradiating them in a research reactor. In addition, valuable radioisotopes can be artifically produced through irradiation of normally stable materials.

The basic function of research reactors—as a source of neutrons and gamma radiation—distinguishes them from power reactors. In general, power reactors utilize the heat produced by fission but not the radiation; research reactors discard the heat but use the radiation. Consequently, the basic design of research reactors is different from that of power reactors.

A common type of research reactor is the pool reactor. This uses a deep pool, in which the water acts as coolant, moderator and shield. The fuel is suspended from a movable bridge across the pool in such a way that the core can be positioned, as desired, in any part of the pool. As a result, experiments can be set up or dismantled at the same time as another experiment is being irradiated in another part of the pool.

Another common type of research reactor is the tank reactor. In this, the tank is as deep as the pool in a pool reactor, but its diameter is just sufficient to accommodate the core, which does not move. Tank reactors may be open at the top, but the more powerful ones have shielding.

The first reactor ever to operate, CP-1, which is shown on

Britain's reactor physics hall at Winfrith, showing four out of the five reactors that are situated in the hall.

LIDO, a pool reactor at Harwell, England. The glow produced is called Cerenkov radiation.

page 18, was graphite moderated, and this is another important type of research reactor. It can use natural uranium as fuel.

Heavy water moderated reactors, which are like top-shielded tank reactors, give a high neutron flux relative to their power level. This is because such reactors use enriched uranium fuel together with, as moderator, heavy water, which has the property of not absorbing neutrons as much as ordinary water.

However, an even greater neutron flux is produced in high flux reactors; these are, of course, thermal neutrons. And a still greater fast neutron flux is produced in a fast reactor like the Dounreay fast reactor (DFR). Although this reactor was originally an experiment in itself, it is also used to irradiate reactor materials. In the DFR the material is subjected in a few months to the radiation it would receive in a lifetime in a thermal reactor.

Recent years have seen the development of pulsed reactors, in which intense bursts of neutrons lasting a fraction of a second are produced.

Despite the variety of types of research reactor, most have experimental facilities that enable them to be used efficiently. These include:

A beam tube—a hollow tube passing through the shielding from near the core, providing a free path for neutrons to pass into experimental equipment outside the reactor.

A thermal column—an opening through the shielding, filled with a moderator to provide a source of thermal neutrons.

A rabbit—a gas or water system for rapidly and easily inserting samples into an area of high flux and moving the sample directly to a laboratory for study when irradiation is complete.

Materials irradiated in research reactors become radioactive and must be handled remotely behind protective shielding.

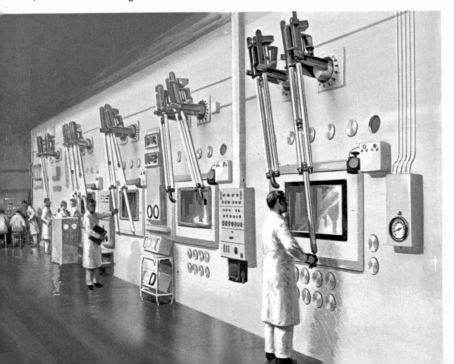

uranium

thorium

Uranium

The average amount of uranium in the earth's crust is between 3 and 4 grams per ton of rock—a vast tonnage of metal. And even though in many deposits the concentration is very low, the economically workable deposits so far discovered are vast—about 680,000 tons. The United States and Canada are the biggest producers in the western world.

The early prospectors for uranium simply went out with Geiger counters to try to detect its radioactivity. Detection of radioactivity is still the basis of uranium survey but, for the rapid exploration of vast areas, it is usually attempted from low-flying aircraft equipped with Geiger counters or scintillation meters and recording equipment. An area suspected of having uranium deposits must be checked in detail by men on foot, equipped with detectors. Further investigations may involve drilling and core-sampling, and mine-opening.

Shallow deposits of uranium are mined by open-cast techniques but underground mines are more common. Whichever way the ore is mined, because of the low uranium content it must be concentrated before it is sent to the refinery to be purified. The ore is concentrated in mills located near the mines. Since uranium ores differ widely, a variety of methods are used. Usually the ore is ground, then the uranium is dissolved out with a suitable reagent—an operation called 'leaching.' Sulphuric acid is often used for leaching, but sometimes sodium carbonate containing some bicarbonate is preferred. Then the uranium is recovered by solvent extraction (a chemical separation method that depends on preferential solubility in different liquids); or by ion exchange, which depends on preferential absorption of solute ions on insoluble resins. It is then roasted to remove excess water. At this point it has become a crude uranium ore concentrate known as 'yellow cake'. In this form it is shipped to the uranium refineries.

The world's uranium and thorium deposits, excluding Russia, China and Eastern Europe (*top*). Open-cast quarrying for ore (*bottom*).

Fuel Manufacture

Uranium must be extremely pure for use in reactors, because any impurities present might absorb neutrons and interfere with the reaction. The refining process varies somewhat from country to country but is basically similar everywhere. The Springfield Works in Great Britain is the largest nuclear fuel factory in the world. Over two million fuel elements have been produced there, on a site that contains refining, conversion and fabrication lines.

The uranium ore concentrate is dissolved in nitric acid to form uranyl nitrate. This is filtered, purified and concentrated, and then sprayed into a 'fluidized bed'. This is a tall, stainless steel vessel containing about ten tons of heated uranium trioxide powder through which a stream of hot compressed air is blown from below. The sprayed uranyl nitrate decomposes to form more uranium trioxide, and as the amount of this increases it overflows to a second fluidized bed; this has hydrogen blown through it and the trioxide is reduced to uranium

A stage in the purification of uranium: uranium ore concentrate is being reduced with magnesium inside the red-hot vessel.

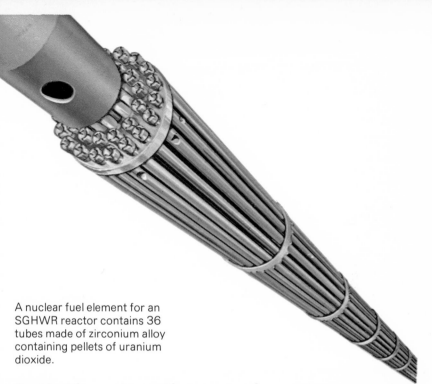

A nuclear fuel element for an SGHWR reactor contains 36 tubes made of zirconium alloy containing pellets of uranium dioxide.

dioxide. The uranium oxide is converted to uranium tetrafluoride, or 'green salt' as it is known, in a third fluidized bed that has hot hydrofluoric acid blown through it.

If the uranium has to be enriched (that is, have its uranium-235 content increased), the tetrafluoride is converted to uranium hexafluoride and transported to the diffusion enrichment plant. For natural uranium metal fuels, however, the tetrafluoride is mixed with magnesium and heated. Molten uranium and slag are produced. The pure uranium billets are remelted and cast into rods which are heat treated, machined, and clad in magnox alloy.

For reactors using oxide fuels, such as the AGRs, the uranium needs to be slightly enriched. It is obtained as uranium hexafluoride from the diffusion plant and converted to uranium dioxide. This is pressed into pellets, which, for AGRs, are inserted into stainless steel tubes and assembled in clusters. The cladding of nuclear fuel is very important. It protects the fuel from corrosion by the reactor coolant, it holds in the radioactive fission products, and it sometimes has a structural function.

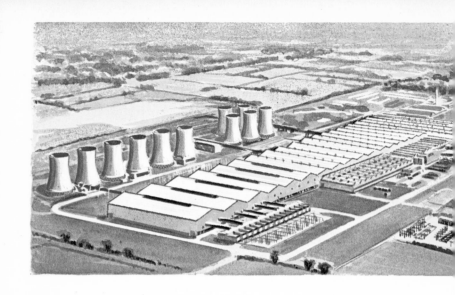

Great Britain's gaseous diffusion plant at Capenhurst, Cheshire

Enrichment

Enriching uranium means increasing the proportion of its U-235 isotope. This is the most difficult step in the production of uranium fuel, because isotopes of the same element are chemically identical. The process must, therefore, be based on a physical property of the isotopes.

Enrichment through the "gaseous diffusion" process relies on the difference in weight of the isotopes. The uranium is processed in the form of uranium hexafluoride, UF_6, which becomes a gas at slightly higher than room temperature. The lighter molecules in the gas are in more rapid random motion than the heavier ones. If, therefore, the mixture of isotopes is in contact with a porous membrane, the lighter isotope hits the membrane more frequently and diffuses through it more quickly than the heavier isotope.

An enrichment plant consists of a series of diffusion stages in a 'cascade'; each stage consists of a chamber divided by a porous membrane. One part of the chamber is at a higher pressure than the other. Entering at the high-pressure end, half the gas diffuses through the membrane—with slightly more $^{235}UF_6$ going through than $^{238}UF_6$; this slightly 'enriched' gas passes to the next stage up the cascade. The half with the reduced $^{235}UF_6$ content is directed to the next stage down the cascade. After many repetitions of the process, the enriched gas is shipped from the plant.

The degree of separation achieved at each stage in the cascade is miniscule, so that hundreds of stages are necessary. As a result, diffusion plants are enormous. They consume as much electricity as a city and are expensive to build—the three plants in the United States cost a total of $24 billion. These plants are at Oak Ridge, Tennessee (the first in the world), Paducah, Kentucky and Portsmouth, Ohio. Great Britain, France, the Soviet Union and China also have diffusion plants. Recently, West Germany perfected a far less costly enrichment technique, involving the use of high-speed centrifuges to separate out the light $^{235}UF_6$ molecules. Small nations will be able to afford this new technology.

How a gaseous diffusion plant works

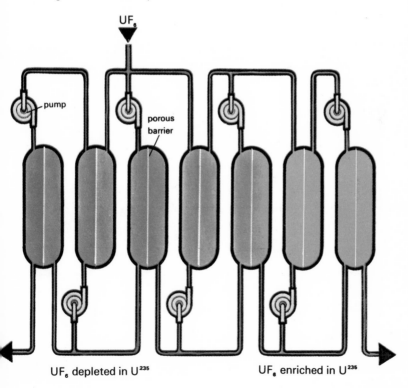

UF_6

pump

porous barrier

UF_6 depleted in U^{235} UF_6 enriched in U^{235}

47

Reprocessing

Nuclear fuel may be in a reactor for several years. Yet when it is removed, only a small percentage of its fissile atoms will have been spent. In fact, it is essential to remove the fuel with much of its fissile content still unused, since radiation damage to the element tends to cause physical distortion and also because fission products soak up neutrons and tend to 'put out' the reaction.

The spent fuel has an obvious value because of its uranium-235 content. In addition, however, some of the uranium-238 will have been converted to plutonium, most of which remains in the spent fuel without undergoing fission. Recovery of these materials is the purpose of reprocessing plants.

The fuel removed from a reactor is, of course, highly radioactive. Although the radioactivity is allowed to partially 'cool off' under water at the reactor site for a period of some months, a reprocessing plant still has to be heavily shielded to handle it. As a result, reprocessing plants must be carefully controlled and are quite complex.

In reprocessing plants, the irradiated fuel is first removed from its container under about 15 feet of water (*right*). The fuel is then dissolved in nitric acid and the fission products removed from this solution by solvent extraction. The uranium and plutonium are then separated and each is purified separately.

Hoisting a flask of irradiated fuel to the dissolver

The British reprocessing plant at Windscale in Cumberland is the biggest in the world. It has a throughput of 2000 metric tons of spent fuel each year. The recovery process at this plant is basically similar to others elsewhere.

At such plants, the purified uranium is depleted of its fissile content, but it still has a use. It is extremely dense (about twice as dense as lead), and can be employed for shielding against radiation in radiographic units in hospitals. It can also be returned to a diffusion plant for re-enrichment, or blended with enriched uranium.

The reprocessing trade is particularly advanced in Britain because the large number of reactors in operation produce a great deal of irradiated fuel. The Windscale plant also handles fuel from overseas. Small reprocessing plants have also been built in the United States, Belgium, France, India and Japan. Several countries are associated through Eurochemic in operating a plant at Mol, in Belgium.

Fuel Cycles

There are numerous ways of using nuclear fuels in various reactors. For instance, natural or enriched uranium may be 'burnt' in a thermal reactor and then discarded. But the spent fuel can also be reprocessed, and its plutonium recycled through thermal reactors. And still other cycles are available that make use of breeder reactors; these cycles may be based on the production of plutonium from uranium-238 in fast reactors or uranium-233 from thorium in thermal reactors.

If the spent fuel is discarded, the number of uranium atoms actually utilized—the 'burn up'—is very low, less than 1 per-

Fast reactors can burn plutonium produced in thermal reactors, and also *breed* more plutonium from depleted and natural uranium.

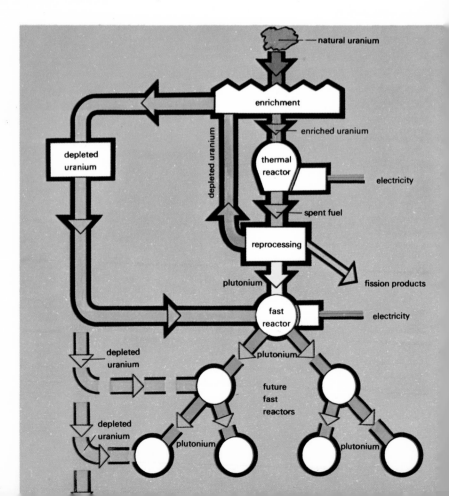

Monazite

cent. Recycling plutonium through thermal reactors improves this percentage but the burn-up is still only a few percent. With fast breeder reactors, however, as much as 75 percent of the uranium can be 'burned'.

Degree of burn-up is not the only factor. Account must be taken of the cost of reactors and plant, of manufacturing the fuel, of reprocessing irradiated fuel, the cost of the fuel actually in reactors, and the time taken for fissile material to double itself in the breeding cycle (the 'doubling time'). Probably the highly efficient fuel cycle of fast breeder reactors will make them the most economic.

Thorium

The most important source of thorium is monazite-bearing sand, which is processed to recover rare earths. It also occurs in some uranium ores.

Thorium for reactor use must be refined to remove all traces of uranium and rare earths. Natural thorium consists of thorium-232, and needs no isotopic 'enriching' process. It does, however, need to be converted to uranium-233 before it is of any use as a nuclear fuel. This might best be done in high-temperature gas-cooled reactors, but it would not produce a breeding gain like that achieved using the uranium-238/plutonium-239 cycle in fast reactors. Commercial converter reactors have not yet been developed, so that the demand for thorium is still low; many known deposits are not yet mined.

Reactor Materials

Atomic energy has produced a demand for a range of materials, sometimes familiar ones processed to a high degree of purity, sometimes unusual ones that were once mere chemical curiosities. They must meet much more stringent specifications than are required in conventional engineering, but in addition to the usual physical properties they must have special nuclear properties. In particular, they must capture few neutrons, so as to avoid interfering with the chain reaction, unless they are control rod materials, for which the ability to capture neutrons must be great. They must also withstand continuous bombardment by neutrons and other radiation for long periods. Two important materials are graphite and heavy water.

Graphite is manufactured by carbonizing petroleum coke, forming the ground carbon with pitch binder, and firing it in several steps at increasing temperatures up to 3000° C. The graphite is then allowed to cool and is eventually machined to the required shape.

Laying blocks of graphite moderator in place during the construction of a power station

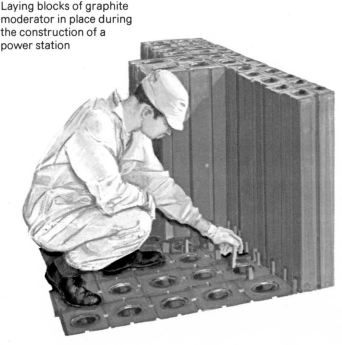

The Connecticut Yankee nuclear generating station in Haddam Neck began operation in 1967. It is owned and operated by the Connecticut Yankee Atomic Power Company and has a capacity of 562 kwe. The reactor is a PWR type.

The production of heavy water involves the separation of isotopes of hydrogen. The masses of these isotopes are far greater in ratio to one another than the isotopes of any other element, and separation is not as difficult as it is for uranium. But it is expensive because of the low proportion (0.015 percent) of heavy water in all naturally occurring water. To produce one pound of heavy water it is necessary to process ten tons of water. There are several different methods. The distillation of liquid hydrogen is a good one (hydrogen boils at $-252.8°C$, deuterium at $-249.7°C$), although it requires considerable knowledge of low-temperature technology. There are several such plants in various parts of the world. In another process, deuterium is made to transfer from hydrogen sulphide to water that is progressively enriched over several stages. Distillation of water has also been used; heavy water boils at $101.42°$ C. Electrolysis is expensive but has been used for the final stages of purification. Light water decomposes faster than heavy water, and the water remaining in the electrolytic cell becomes more concentrated in heavy water.

Gross Generating Capacity (MW) (Megawatts: one million watts of electric power) by mid-1968

Britain 4850
United States 2900
Russia 1500
France 1100
Italy 630
West Germany 320
Canada 225
Japan 180
Czechoslovakia 110
Belgium 11.4
Sweden 10

The world's nuclear power stations. None exist as yet in the southern hemisphere.

REACTORS AT WORK

Nuclear Power around the World

By far the most important use of nuclear reactors is in the generation of electricity. In this, nuclear power is no longer merely something 'of the future'—it is established.

It is particularly well established in Britain where an early start was made because of the cost of fossil fuel and because large quantities of oil have to be imported. A long-term concept of three generations of nuclear systems was initiated: the Calder Hall type of gas-cooled reactor burning natural uranium, followed by advanced gas-cooled reactors (AGR) burn-

ing slightly enriched uranium, followed by fast reactors fueled with the plutonium produced by the other reactors. A construction program of the first type totaling 5000 MW is complete, the last station (Wylfa, in Anglesey) coming on power in 1969. These stations have, like Calder Hall and its twin, Chapelcross, operated extremely reliably. Well over 100,000 million kWh (kilowatt-hours) of electricity have been generated — more than in the rest of the world put together. A second construction program, of 8000 MW, of AGRs is under way. Finally, the fast reactor program is well advanced, with the 250 MW (e) prototype under construction at Dounreay; it will reach full power in 1971 and pave the way for the larger versions coming into use later in the 1970's.

A change in the basic plan is still possible; high-temperature gas-cooled reactors could be introduced, or heavy water reactors like the steam-generating heavy water reactor at Winfrith. A feature of the British nuclear power programs has been the steady fall in costs with each station built. From Berkeley (the first of the Calder Hall type) to Oldbury, which came on power in 1967, the cost of the electricity produced fell by 45 percent. The stage has been reached where nuclear power is competitive with coal.

The fall in costs has been due partly to advances in tech-

Hunterston 'B' nuclear power station, a twin-AGR station under construction in Scotland. It will produce 1250 MW of electricity.

nology and partly to the increase in the size of the plants. The second factor has been particularly true in the United States. The vast supplies of cheap coal, oil and natural gas there had meant that nuclear power was not urgently required. Only small government-assisted plants were built until the mid-1960's. Then, in 1964, the General Electric Company sold a BWR to Jersey Central Power and Light Company—the 515 MW (e) plant for Oyster Creek—which was competitive with coal. Since then there has been an avalanche of orders, many of the plants ordered being much larger than Oyster Creek. Although few of them have been as competitive as Oyster Creek, the demand for electricity in the United States (its

200 million people use three times as much power per head as people in Britain) ensures a steady expansion of the nuclear power industry.

American PWRs and BWRs have been exported to several countries. However, when they were compared with the AGR in the tenders for Dungeness 'B', the power from the AGR turned out to be cheaper by 10 percent.

The competition between these reactor types has still to be settled in France. There, despite the existence of a number of gas-cooled reactors, the electricity generating board is also interested in the light water reactors. An interesting feature of nuclear power in France is the cooperative ventures with neigh-

San Onofre, a 429 MW PWR in California. Much of the equipment can be left in the open because of the climate.

boring countries. One gas-cooled power station is being built on the Spanish side of the frontier, and the power will be shared between the two countries. A PWR has been built jointly with Belgium, on the French side of the border at Chooz. Other projects involve Germany and Switzerland. France started building a 250 MW(e) fast reactor in 1969.

Italy took a different road to nuclear power by gaining experience with nuclear power stations of foreign design. A British-designed gas-cooled power station was built at Latina and an American PWR and a BWR were constructed at Trino Vercellere and Gargliano, respectively.

Building a typical nuclear power station

Erecting
structural
steelwork for
the power hall

Installing
banks of
feeder tubes
that lead to
the boiling
channels
in the
reactor core

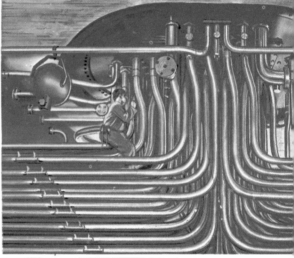

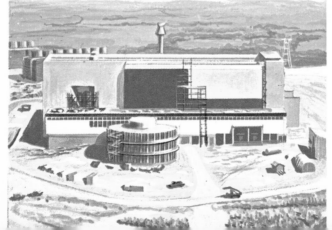

The
construction
nears
completion.

The interior of the completed reactor building with the turbo-alternator in the foreground and the reactor area in the background.

Checking the fuel channels in the reactor for accuracy of construction

Loading the fuel into the reactor

Germany also has bought American know-how on light water reactors. But it has also developed a heavy water reactor (and exported one to Argentina) and intends to build two fast reactor prototypes: one steam-cooled, the other cooled by liquid sodium.

Nuclear power is essential to Sweden, where 95 percent of the electricity is produced by hydroelectric schemes that cannot be developed much further. Sweden is, however, almost completely self-sufficient, having developed its own pressurized heavy water reactors and boiling heavy water reactors. They have not yet reached the competitive stage though, and a BWR, developed after some collaboration with the United States, may be used for at least part of Sweden's large program of reactor construction.

Heavy water reactors are well established in Canada. A 200 MW(e) plant is in operation at Douglas Point, and a 1000 MW (e) plant with two reactors is being built at Pickering. Canada has also exported heavy water reactors to India and Pakistan.

The first large nuclear power station in Asia was built at Tokai Mura, in Japan. It is a British design, with a capacity of 160 MW(e). Since then Japan has also built BWRs and PWRs based on American designs, but is determined to develop its own nuclear industry to maximum self-sufficiency. It intends to develop a heavy water reactor, probably similar to the British SGHWR (on which it has already bought some know-how) and also a fast reactor. Of the other Asian countries only India

Four nuclear power stations have been built by L'Electricité de France on the banks of the River Loire at Chinon in France.

Irradiated fuel is transported from the Latina power station in Italy for reprocessing at Windscale in Britain. The fuel is contained in lead-lined vessels aboard a special ship that is refrigerated to remove the heat produced by the fuel.

and Pakistan have 'gone nuclear'. Apart from its Canadian reactor, India is also building an American-designed BWR.

With its immense reserves of oil and coal, Russia has not felt the need to introduce nuclear power very quickly. But the problems of building and operating other kinds of power stations in the more remote areas of Arctic or desert regions have caused them to develop their own PWRs and water-cooled graphite-moderated reactors. For instance, one plant, with six reactors of the latter type, is situated in Siberia. The first large PWR, with an output of 210 MW(e) was built at Novovoronezh on the River Don; it was commissioned in 1964. Others are being built. Russia also has a large fast breeder program, with a 250 MW(e) reactor (BN350) under construction at Shevchenko on the Caspian Sea. Larger versions are to be introduced in the early 1970's.

The power programs of most of the eastern European countries have depended upon Russia. For instance, Czechoslovakia has a Russian-designed gas-cooled heavy water reactor at Bohunice and East Germany has a Russian PWR. However, Romania and Yugoslavia might use Western reactor designs.

World-Wide Nuclear Power

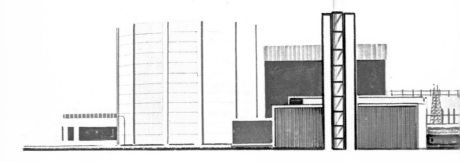

Douglas Point, Lake Huron, Ontario, Canada; a 200 MW heavy water reactor

Rhajasthan, India; a 400 MW Canadian-designed heavy water reactor

Novoronezh, Russia (*above*); a 210 MW PWR. The dome at the bottom is the cover for the reactor.

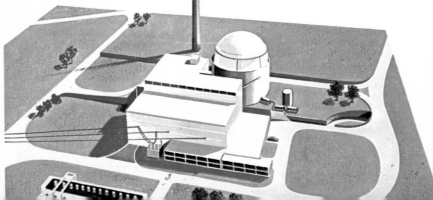

Latina, Italy; a 200 MW gas-cooled reactor of British design

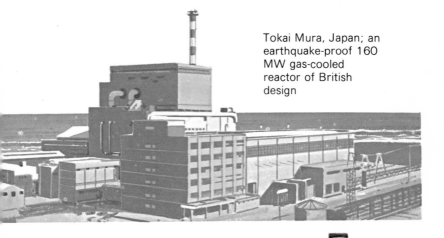

Tokai Mura, Japan; an earthquake-proof 160 MW gas-cooled reactor of British design

Bohunice, Czechoslovakia; a 150 MW gas-cooled heavy water reactor of Russian design

Desalination

Producing a pound of bread requires 300 gallons of water; a pound of beef, 3,000 gallons; and an automobile, 500,000 gallons. Industrial demands like these, together with requirements for household supplies, are stimulating efforts to develop new sources of water supply. One of these will be the nuclear-powered desalination plant.

Plants for desalination—making potable water from sea water—have been built in various parts of the world, most of them relying on distillation and obtaining their heat by burning coal or oil. Other processes are also used, such as electrodialysis and reverse osmosis, but distillation is of particular interest here because of the possibility of using the waste heat from nuclear reactors to evaporate the water.

In the most widely used version of the distillation process—multistage 'flash distillation'—the hot brine is pumped through a series of chambers, each at a lower pressure than the

Multistage flash distillation

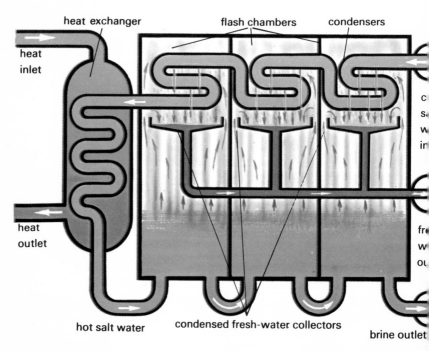

heat exchanger · flash chambers · condensers

heat inlet

heat outlet

hot salt water · condensed fresh-water collectors · brine outlet

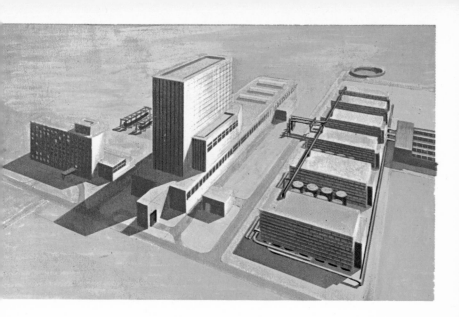

An impression of a nuclear-powered desalination plant

previous one. In each chamber some of the brine rapidly evaporates, or 'flashes'. The steam condenses on tubes cooled by the incoming brine and the condensate—very pure water—is collected and pumped from the plant. The brine fed into the plant warms up as it passes through the tubes and is heated further before it enters the distillation chambers.

The cheapest form of heat for this process is the waste heat of power stations. In a modern coal- or oil-fired power station, and also in an AGR, only about 40 percent of the heat produced is converted to electricity; the other 60 percent is wasted as low-temperature steam. The plant is said to have an efficiency of 40 percent.

For a desalination plant, slightly more than just the waste heat is needed and some electricity production is lost. But nearly all the heat produced by the power station may be put to use.

A nuclear powered desalination plant could not at the moment be built to produce water at a low enough price for purely agricultural use. However, for industrial and domestic uses the price is acceptable in some countries, including the United States. In fact, a nuclear desalination plant is planned for a man-made island (Bolsa Island) off the coast of southern California.

The *Otto Hahn,* Germany's
nuclear-powered ore carrier

Nuclear Propulsion

The compact nature of nuclear fuel inevitably made it attractive for propelling ships, and it was in 1954 that the American nuclear submarine *Nautilus* was launched. It was the first vessel in a huge nuclear fleet, which now includes submarines, destroyers, cruisers and an aircraft carrier. They all use PWRs. Russia also has nuclear submarines, and so have Great Britain and France.

The American nuclear-powered passenger-cargo vessel *Savannah* completed her sea trials in 1962. She displaces 22,000 tons and is powered by a PWR that delivers 22,000 shaft horse power; her cruising speed is 21 knots. In a series of demonstration visits to various parts of the world, the *Savannah* traveled 90,000 miles and burned only 35 pounds of U-235.

The Russian icebreaker *Lenin,* in polar seas

The nuclear ship *Savannah,* American cargo-passenger ship

The *Savannah's* fuel can last three years before it needs to be replaced. Although the *Savannah* is not competitive with other merchant ships, it could pave the way for vessels that will be.

The potential economic advantages of nuclear propulsion for commercial vessels are higher cruising speed, infrequent refueling and more available cargo space. But the capital costs of nuclear propulsion reactors are such that the most likely vessels to become economic at present are bulk cargo ships, such as ore carriers and oil tankers. The Germans recently launched a ship of this type, the nuclear-powered ore carrier *Otto Hahn.* The PWR in this ship is a much improved version of the one used in the *Savannah.*

Russia is using nuclear propulsion in a way that will bring economic benefit. Since 1959, the nuclear-powered icebreaker *Lenin* has operated in polar regions. Two sister ships are planned for 1971. The aim is to keep open the sea route right across the Arctic Ocean all the year round. Convoys of ships would then sail north of Siberia from Murmansk to Vladivostok, some 5,800 miles. The Suez Canal route is 13,000 miles.

Several other countries, including Great Britain, Japan, Sweden, Norway, the Netherlands and Italy, may eventually build nuclear ships. Other forms of transport, large hovercraft, for instance, may eventually be nuclear powered.

67

The generating hall at the Ågesta power station, Sweden

Small Power Reactors

Nuclear power as discussed previously concerned large reactors, but small power reactors producing less than 100 MW(e), (megawatts of electricity) could have important roles to play in both the developing and the industrialized countries. There are, in fact, a number of small reactors already in use around the world.

In the developing countries, most of the power stations being installed are in unit sizes less than 100 MW(e), and even in countries such as Germany and Italy 20 to 30 percent of the new generating plants are in small units. For small reactors to be introduced in large numbers they would have to be competitive. In the developing countries in particular this will be difficult because they tend to have satisfactory natural resources — much of the power is produced by hydroelectric plants. The most successful small reactors so far have been in very remote areas such as the Arctic and Antarctic.

However, two interesting small reactors have been in use for some time near centers of population. One, the Ågesta reactor, supplies heat to the Farsta suburb of Stockholm. It is a pressurized heavy water reactor producing 125 MW of heat; part of this is converted to 35 MW of electricity and the rest—70 MW of heat—is available as hot water from the turbine exhaust.

The other one is the Norwegian Halden reactor, which produces steam for a paper factory. This reactor is the boiling heavy water type, using natural uranium fuel. The reactor is built into a cavern hollowed out of the mountainside. Heavy water steam is produced and passed to a heat exchanger where it boils ordinary water to produce the process steam. The capacity of the plant is 10 MW of heat.

In Britain, waste steam from Calder Hall has been used for many years at the adjacent Windscale site. In fact, the provision of heat for industrial processes is the likely use of small reactors if they ever do become competitive. Small high-temperature gas-cooled reactors might have a future in processes such as steelmaking.

A competitive small reactor will have considerable potential in industrial complexes, but there are already situations in which portable reactors are superior to fossil-fueled power

Loading one section of a portable nuclear power plant for transport to a remote site

stations. Indeed, they may be the only possible power system.

For instance, the United States has used nuclear reactors at its bases at Camp Century in Greenland and Mc-Murdo Sound in Antarctica. The reactors and other components had to be transported in a number of packages by ship or plane. Not only had the power plants to be small enough for these transports, they also had to be easy to assemble at the remote bases. Oil-fired plants could have been installed in these places, but they would have required a regular supply of oil, and refueling would have been necessary even during the worst weather conditions. For the nuclear plants, refueling is required only once every year or two, and even then the new fuel is easily flown to the site in a small package.

Portable reactors are classified as low power (up to 1 MW), medium power (1 to 10 MW) and high power (over 10 MW). The two portable plants described are each 1.5 MW units. Other portable plants have been built or are under construction, most

Installing a portable reactor at the American base at McMurdo Sound, Antractica. The operators are dressed much like surgeons to reduce the amount of dirt getting into the reactor.

70

of them being miniaturized PWRs. Reduction in size has been achieved mainly by packing boilers, valves and pipes into small packages, because the size of the reactor itself cannot be reduced by much. The need for the plant to be compact, plus the requirements for reliability, safety and portability, has meant that the cost of the power produced has not been the only factor considered.

Despite the compactness and portability of the plants just described, it might take over 60 days to assemble them. Even more time is spent excavating the site. Yet there are occasions when power is needed instantly. For example, when earthquakes, hurricanes or floods have disrupted the power supplies to large areas, the great need is for a mobile nuclear power plant to restore power to the disaster area. The United States has a mobile reactor, capable of providing 10 MW of electricity, already in service. It is mounted aboard a converted Liberty Boat and can move to a disaster area and quickly supply power, thereby aiding the recovery of the area. Other plants are planned which will be mounted on trucks and trailers. They will be able to produce power within six hours of moving to the disaster area. Since they might quickly be needed elsewhere they are designed to be on the road again within twelve hours if necessary.

Instant power—a small nuclear power plant mounted on a truck.

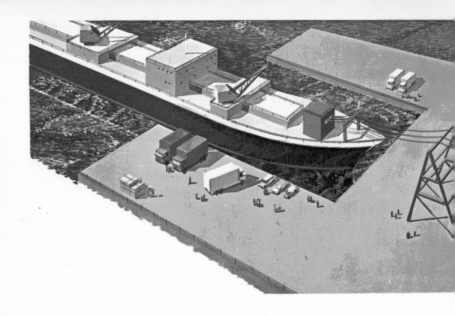

A ship-borne nuclear
power plant can supply
power to disaster
areas.

These plants will be much lighter than the portable plants described above, weighing less than 50 short tons (a portable plant might weigh about 500 short tons).

Russia has also developed a mobile plant. It consists of two units mounted on tracks, and it can cross rough terrain. It can also be dismantled and transported by air. The capacity of the plant is 1.5 MW, and its water-cooled and moderated reactor needs to be refueled only every five years. It is not intended to be used solely as a temporary or emergency supply; it could, for example, be used on remote construction sites.

One other application of small-scale nuclear power could become important—its use on the sea bed. It is difficult to imagine large-scale operations underwater without concluding that the source of power should be nuclear. Reactors could well become the source of heat for large-scale sea farming in nutrient-rich waters. Or they could provide the power needed to extract minerals from the rich underwater deposits known to exist.

Reactors in Space

On April 3, 1965, a satellite carrying a nuclear reactor was placed in orbit by the United States 800 miles above the earth. The first reactor in space was called SNAP 10A. SNAP stands for Systems for Nuclear Auxiliary Power. The 500-watt SNAP 10A functioned successfully for 43 days.

A satellite needs electricity for the purification and regeneration of water and air, for instruments and radios, and to keep the cabin at the right temperature. For long space journeys, other sources of energy, such as batteries, are unsuitable, basically because they do not have sufficient energy per unit mass; and solar energy is unsuitable for spacecraft traveling very far away from the sun.

The United States has, therefore, a long-term development program for SNAP generators. This includes the possible use of thermionic power generation, the building of miniature high-speed turbines, and the use of liquid-metal coolants. The coolant in SNAP 10A was a mixture of sodium and potassium

Nuclear reactors will supply power for manned orbital laboratories. The reactor is situated at the far left, well away from the crew.

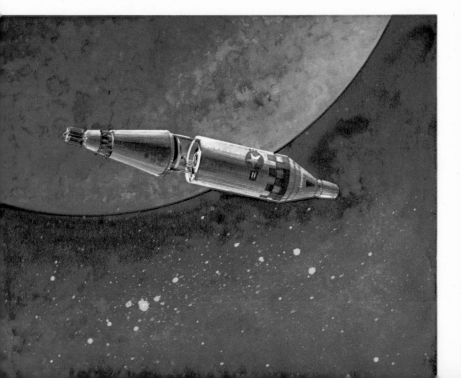

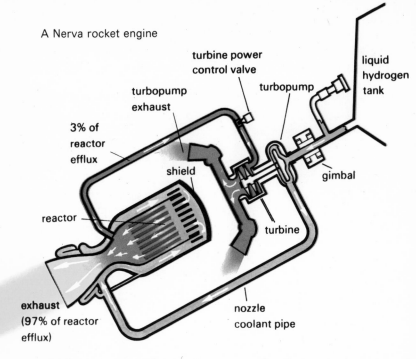

A Nerva rocket engine

turbine power
control valve

liquid
hydrogen
tank

turbopump
exhaust

turbopump

3% of
reactor
efflux

shield

gimbal

reactor

turbine

exhaust
(97% of reactor
efflux)

nozzle
coolant pipe

which was pumped past thermocouples that converted the heat to electricity.

As well as developing SNAP units, which will eventually provide electricity for orbiting stations and lunar bases, as well as for long-distance satellites, the United States is also investigating nuclear rocket engines.

In an ordinary chemical rocket, the hot gases produced by combustion are ejected from the throat of the nozzle and expand against its flared sides, pushing the rocket upward. Similarly, in a nuclear rocket, the thrust is produced by hot gases (heated in a nuclear reactor) expanding against the reactor nozzle, but the exhaust velocity of the gas is twice that of the gas from the chemical rocket. The result is that the nuclear rocket can give the same level of thrust for half the amount of propellent, and the weight saved in this way permits a much greater payload to be carried.

The American project for a nuclear rocket, project 'Rover', has reached the stage where a number of reactors have been ground-tested. These are graphite moderated and use hydrogen as coolant (or propellent). The present aim is to develop an engine, NERVA-1, which would produce 1500 MW of heat and a thrust of 65,000 to 75,000 pounds; it should fly in 1975.

The basic components of a nuclear rocket engine are illustrated. The reactor in the NERVA engine must reach a temperature above 2000° C. It is hotter than any earth-bound power station but operates for less than an hour. Superhot hydrogen leaves the nozzle at supersonic speeds. To enable the nozzle to withstand this it is cooled with supercooled hydrogen passing to the reactor from the fuel tanks.

Although the nuclear rocket engine is considerably heavier than the chemical one, it will be useful for long journeys in weightless space, where the extra mass will not increase the need for fuel. The NERVA-1 engine is intended for instrumental interplanetary probes.

Manned interplanetary rockets
will be powered by several
nuclear engines.

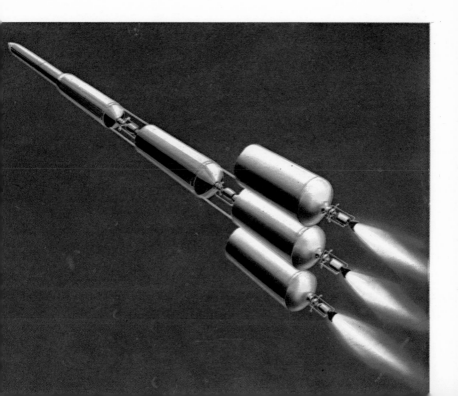

RADIOISOTOPES

Making Radioisotopes

The manufacture of radioactive isotopes, or radioisotopes, is now a thriving industry, with their use in medicine, industry, agriculture and science firmly established. About $7 million worth of radioisotopes are sold annually by Britain's Radiochemical Center alone.

Making a radioisotope generally means altering the nucleus of a stable element. This is done by striking it with a neutron, a proton, an alpha particle or a deuteron. The nucleus may absorb the impinging particle and emit excess energy as a gamma radiation, a neutron, a proton or an alpha particle. To produce such nuclear reactions, protons, deuterons and alpha particles must be accelerated to high speeds to overcome the electrical repulsion of the nucleus. Neutrons, being neutral, are not repelled.

Ionized particles can be accelerated to penetration energies by a cyclotron. The path of a charged particle in a magnetic field is curved; this effect is put to use in the cyclotron, which

Nuclear reactors are used to make radioisotopes. They are transported in small trolleys for further processing.

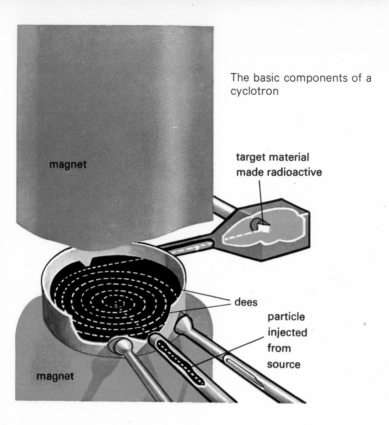

The basic components of a cyclotron

magnet

target material made radioactive

dees

particle injected from source

magnet

has an electromagnet. Between the poles of the magnet are two flat D-shaped hollow chambers, known as 'dees'. A vacuum exists within the chambers. An electric arc ionizes the hydrogen, deuterium or helium atoms, producing positively charged protons, deuterons or alpha particles. A high-frequency alternating current is fed across the dees; it accelerates the ions, and the magnetic field makes them travel in a spiral path away from the center. By the time the ions reach the edge of the dees, they are traveling at a very high speed indeed. Radioisotopes can be produced by placing suitable stable material in the path of the ionic beam.

The most convenient source of neutrons is a nuclear reactor. The radioisotopes produced this way have excess neutrons. Cyclotron-produced radioisotopes may also have excess neutrons, or they may be neutron deficient. But because reactors are convenient to use, cyclotrons are generally reserved only for the latter type of radioisotope.

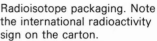

Radioisotope packaging. Note the international radioactivity sign on the carton.

Radioisotopes can be obtained from nuclear reactors in another way; when the uranium-235 is fissioned, it breaks up in a variety of reactions, yielding a complex mixture of radio-isotopes. These can be extracted when the spent fuel is re-processed for plutonium recovery. Strontium-90 and caesium-137 are obtained in this way.

Usually a radioisotope produced in a cyclotron or reactor must be further processed before it can be used. This often involves difficult chemical operations which must be carried out behind shielding. The final problem is distribution to the customer and concerns half-life. Long-lived radioisotopes, such as carbon-14, can be held in stock, but short-lived radio-isotopes, such as phosphorus-32 or gold-198, must be manu-factured continuously, depending upon the half-life of the isotope and the demands that are made for it.

Handling radioisotopes

A Geiger counter (*left*) and a
scintillation counter (*below*)

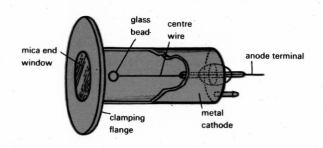

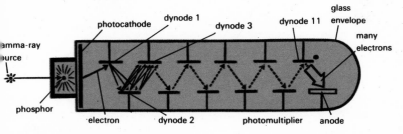

Measuring Radioactivity

Alpha and beta particles ionize molecules in gases through which they pass; the number of positive and negative ions produced is a measure of the amount of radiation that has passed through the gas. The ionization makes the gas electrically conducting, and this effect is utilized in a number of radiation detectors or counters.

A Geiger counter, for instance, has two electrodes. Radiation enters through a window and ionizes gas between the electrodes, causing a current to flow between them. A single particle entering the chamber will set off ionization, which builds up into an 'avalanche'. The pulse of electricity can then be counted or recorded.

Scintillation counters detect and count the flashes of light produced when radiation falls on a phosphor. The light is converted into electrons by a photocathode, and the electrons amplified into measurable impulses by a photomultiplier tube. Radioactivity can also be detected by its effect on a photographic plate or film.

Radioisotopes in Medicine

Among the first people to use radioisotopes were medical research workers. They were quick to realize that radioisotopes were convenient for studying the complexities of body chemistry, by serving as radioactive *tracers*. A radioactive tracer is a chemical in which some of the atoms are made radioactive. Chemically it is indistinguishable from the non-radioactive material, but it can be followed in its passage through the body by means of suitable radiation detectors. For example, a molecule of hemoglobin carrying a radioactive iron atom is still hemoglobin and it behaves in the body the way hemoglobin should behave. The radioisotope iron-59, which emits beta particles and gamma rays, has been used in this way in studies of blood formation. A small amount is injected into the patient's body and finds its way to the bone marrow, where new blood cells are made. The build-up of new blood containing the iron-59 can be followed by detecting the gamma rays that

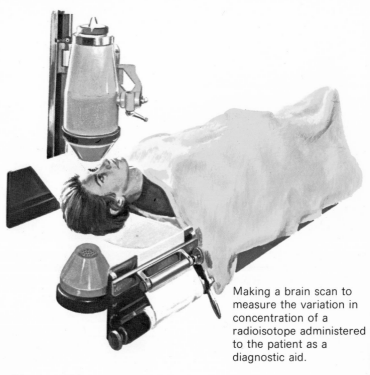

Making a brain scan to measure the variation in concentration of a radioisotope administered to the patient as a diagnostic aid.

are given off. Other chemical constituents of the body can also be tracked in this way.

Radioisotopes are also used in medical diagnosis. One particularly valuable technique is radioisotope scanning. For this the patient is given the radioisotope in a chemical form that causes its concentration in the organ to be studied. The radiation can be tracked photographically or by electronic scanning equipment. Any abnormally large or small uptake of the radioactively labeled chemicals can be detected. The technique can also be used to confirm the absence of any abnormality. This technique is especially useful in locating brain tumors. The radioisotope used is mercury-197, in a chemical that concentrates in the brain. By making scans at right angles the surgeon can find the exact location of the brain tumor. Radioisotope scanning can also detect bone cancers that would not appear on an X-radiograph; for this, radioactive fluorine is used. To detect lung abnormalities, albumin labeled with technetium-99 is used. The albumin is coagulated into small lumps which, when injected into the patient, are carried along in the bloodstream. The particles are small enough to be

X-ray photographs may be superimposed on radiation scan pictures to help locate brain tumors. A normal head is shown (*left*) and a diseased head (*right*), with side views (*above*) and front views (*below*). The dark area indicates a tumor.

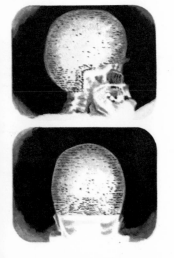 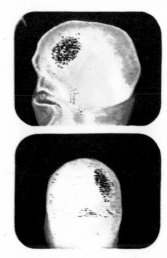

trapped in the very narrow blood vessels inside the lung, and the radiation emitted can be detected. An area of abnormal tissue will have a reduced blood supply and, therefore, a smaller quantity of radioisotope.

There is one other important medical use for radioisotopes, which has been established for some years. This is radiotherapy, the use of high-energy radiation in medical treatment. It is generally associated with the treatment of cancer, although it has other uses. The amount of radioactivity employed is much greater than in diagnosis, but it is accurately computed to give the maximum therapeutic effect without harming healthy tissues. As a treatment for cancer, it generally improves the chances of recovery of the patient. It works by destroying the cells in the cancer, or at least damaging them and preventing them from multiplying.

Basically, there are two ways in which the treatment is carried out; either by using a long-lived radioisotope externally several times or by introducing a short-lived radioisotope into the body or into the diseased tissue itself. The first method, *teletherapy,* was the earliest method used. X-rays were employed and quite often they still are. Where a radioisotope is

Equipment used for radiotherapy

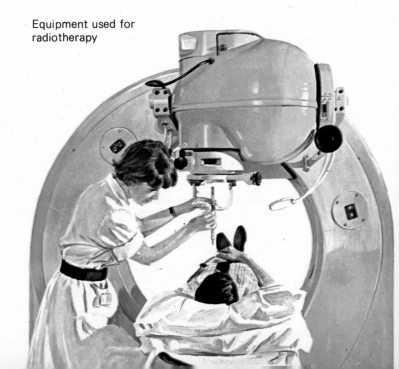

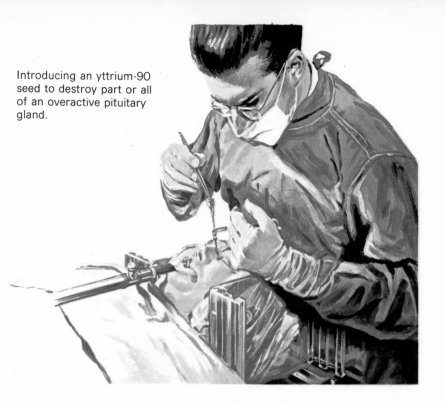

Introducing an yttrium-90 seed to destroy part or all of an overactive pituitary gland.

used it is generally a large amount of a gamma-emitter such as cobalt-60. To avoid injuring healthy tissue a number of doses are given from different angles, with the dose at the tumor building up each time. The equipment usually consists of a source mounted so that it can rotate about the patient's body.

Radiation sources can also be planted in the tumor. Radium needles have long been used for this, and gold-198 and cobalt-60 seeds are also employed. Much smaller doses are required with this treatment.

Another therapeutical technique locates the radiation source in the diseased organ by choosing a chemical that concentrates in the organ. Iodine-131, for instance, which concentrates in the thyroid, can be used to treat an overactive thyroid. Phosphorus-32, administered orally, is used to treat a type of blood cancer in which a proliferation of red blood cells is produced; it slows down their formation. Finally, applicators containing beta-emitters can be placed against the skin to cure skin cancer.

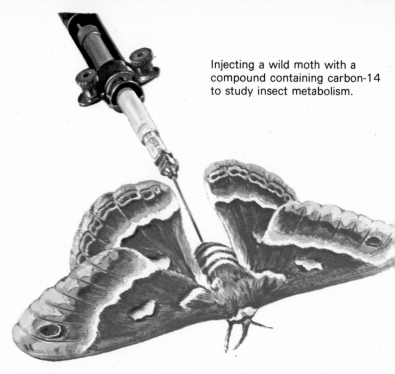

Injecting a wild moth with a compound containing carbon-14 to study insect metabolism.

Radioisotopes in Agriculture

Radioisotopes are now very improtant to the farmer, not as something used directly on crops, but in several other ways. For instance, radioactive tracers have been used to study fertilizers and mineral metabolism in plants. Fertilizers labeled with phosphorus-32 have been used to measure the availability of phosphate in the soil and the uptake of phosphorus by plants. Radioisotopes have also been used extensively in the study of the biochemistry and metabolism of food-producing animals. Better methods of feeding, for better production, have been developed.

Radiation is helping to eradicate insect pests. The method used — the 'sterile male' technique — involves rearing insects in mass and sterilizing them by controlled irradiation while they are immature, followed by the dispersal of the insects over the infested area. The unproductive mating of sterile males and wild females eventually leads to the eradication of the species. The method presents no hazard to man or other living organisms, as the insects are not contaminated by the radiation. The sterile male technique has been used to rid Capri of Mediter-

Monitoring a plant fed with fertilizer containing phosphorus-32 to find out how the plant uses the fertilizer.

ranean fruit flies, which used to damage the citrus crops and other fruits. The oriental fruit fly has been eradicated from Guam and other islands in the Marianas group. Other pests against which the technique might be used are the screw-worm fly (a cattle pest), the codling moth (a fruit pest) and the gypsy moth, which feeds on the leaves of fruit and forest trees.

World food supplies will soon be benefiting from new strains of plants produced by mutation—a change in the inheritance of plant characteristics—induced by radiation. The new plants include early maturing soybean and better yielding rice in Japan, larger and early ripening peach in Argentina, and high-protein wheat in India. The Argentine peach was produced by chronic exposure of growing trees to gamma radiation; and the Indian wheat, by a combination of exposure of seeds to ultraviolet and gamma radiation.

Radiation can also be used to prevent wastage of grain during storage; controlled irradiation is used to kill or sterilize the insects in it, thereby reducing their overall population throughout the grain.

Radioisotopes in Industry

Radioisotopes have proved to be extremely useful in industry and, used with suitable detectors, are now employed in many processes.

One of the earliest uses of radioisotopes was in radiography, with the more familiar X-ray machine being replaced by a gamma-emitter such as cobalt-60 (which is a very powerful one) or caesium-137, iridium-192 or thulium-170 (which are much less powerful). As in X-radiography, the rays passing through the object being examined produce an image on X-ray film. However, the radioactive source is more portable than the much more bulky and heavy X-ray machine, even though the source must be kept in a thick lead container when not in use. Gamma radiography has long been the accepted method of testing welds in cross-country pipelines, and the source can easily be maneuvered into the right position to radiograph a component of an assembled machine. It is much slower than X-radiography; a radiograph obtainable in seconds with an X-ray machine may take several hours with gamma rays. Quite often, however, this is put to good use and the source left in position (probably at the center of a ring of objects being radiographed) overnight in a locked room or cellar. Each object will have its own container of film on which the image is recorded.

Radiography is one of several techniques that allow the product of an industry to be tested without damaging it in any

A radioisotope gauge used in the packaging industry to measure the thickness of polyethelene and cardboard for waterproofing cartons.

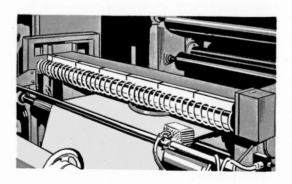

Using gamma rays to radiograph a weld seam in a pressure vessel.

way. Another relies on the attenuation of beta particles as they pass through material; the thickness of the material can be determined, and thickness gauges based on this principle can also be used to feed back signals to the production plant to control the thickness of the material to a desired value. Materials produced in this way include many kinds of paper and metals, vinyl wall coverings, surgical adhesive, tire fabric, rubber, asbestos, galvanized zinc, floor coverings, adhesives and sandpaper. With many of these materials the sheet rushes past the gauge at hundrds of feet per minute.

Density gauges working on a similar principle are used to

Gamma radiography was used at Stonehenge to measure the depth of a crack found in one of the stones.

measure and control the production and manufacture of a similar range of materials.

Another kind of gauge uses the gamma rays back-scattered from the coated surface of a tube to measure the thickness of the coating on the tube, or the thickness of the tube wall or other surfaces where only one side is accessible. This type of gauge can also be used to find out how much rusting has occurred on steel girders.

A problem in several industries is checking whether packages have been filled properly. Here again, radioisotope instruments are used. The source is placed beneath the moving line of packages, with a detector above, and any wrongly filled packages are ejected from the production line. Cans of beer and other liquid levels can be checked by radioisotopes. The gauges employed measure the level of the liquid in each can, and any that are not correctly filled are thrown off the production line.

The level of liquid in large containers can be found in a similar way; for instance, the level of liquid carbon dioxide in cylinders used for fire extinguishing can be easily checked, and corrosive liquids or others under high pressure and totally en-

A radioisotope gauge for measuring the level of liquid in a container

A radioisotope gauge for checking that packages are properly filled

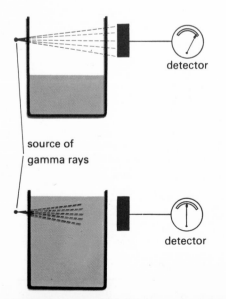

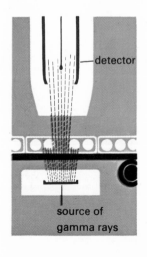

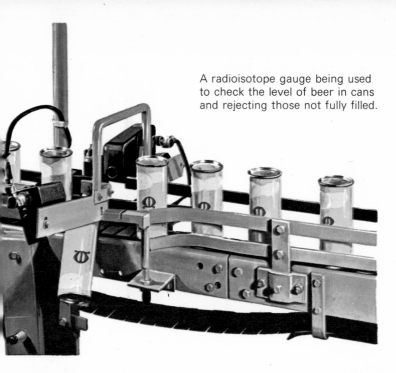

A radioisotope gauge being used to check the level of beer in cans and rejecting those not fully filled.

closed in sealed containers are particularly good examples of fluids that are conveniently controlled by these gauges. The height of molten metal in blast furnaces has been checked by the gamma rays from cobalt-60. Monitoring and controlling the height of molten glass in the feed from a glass furnace is another use of this type of gauge.

Many industries use mixing processes, and tracers have been used to determine just how efficient some of these processes are. An example is the food industry. When radioisotopes are used in food they must have short half-lives. Manganese-56 (half-life 2.6 hours) and sodium-24 (15 hours) are very suitable. But even though these are used only in small amounts and soon decay, the samples of food tested are not released to the consumer.

In some industries the movement of material in bulk has been investigated with tracers. Plants for manufacturing fertilizers, cement and glass have been tested and their conditions of operation adjusted for best performance.

The detection of leaks in pipelines is relatively easy with radioisotopes. A radioisotope, such as sodium-24, is pumped along the pipeline, followed, about half a mile behind, by a

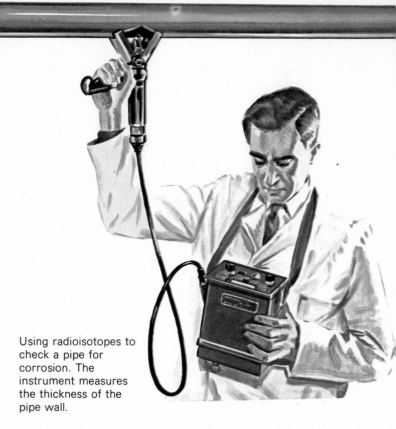

Using radioisotopes to check a pipe for corrosion. The instrument measures the thickness of the pipe wall.

self-contained detector unit attached to a 'go-devil'. Besides a Geiger counter the detector carries a miniature wire recorder. At the point of the leak some of the tracer solution will have been left in the soil, and when the detector passes it the Geiger counter registers an increase in radioactivity, which will be recorded. When the detector is recovered, the position of the leak can be determined.

Tracers have also been used on a large scale for following the movement of sand under the sea and mud on beds of rivers. This has led, for instance, in an investigation of the Firth of Forth in Scotland, to the discovery that dredged mud was being dumped in a channel from which it was almost immediately carried upstream; an ebb channel was tried, and tracers were then used to prove that the mud was being carried out to sea.

An interesting use was found for radioisotopes in the con-

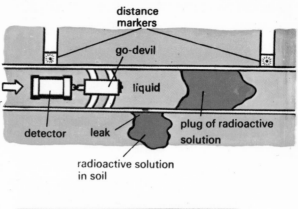

Detecting a leak in a pipe. A detector pulled by a 'go-devil' follows a plug of radioisotope along the pipe. The detector contains a recorder that produces a graph (*below*). The small peak shows a leak in the pipe and the large peaks indicate the distance markers, enabling the position of the leak to be determined.

distance markers

go-devil

liquid

detector   leak

plug of radioactive solution

radioactive solution in soil

struction of Sydney Opera House. This unique structure uses concrete reinforced with steel cables. The problem was to locate voids between the set concrete and the steel cables, because, if these were not filled in, corrosion would have occurred. Sodium carbonate-24 solution was pumped up between the strands of steel hawsers which run through the middle of the concrete cells. Scientists with portable scintillation counters climbed into the scaffolding to check for pockets of radioactive fluids. The voids were then filled in with concrete.

Radioactivity enables the wear on machinery to be accurately and quickly measured. The wear on the gear of a car

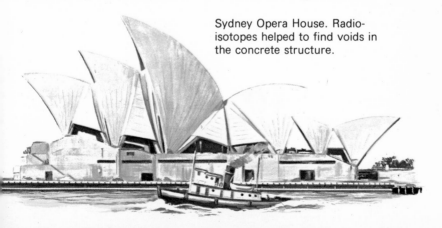

Sydney Opera House. Radioisotopes helped to find voids in the concrete structure.

caused by as little as ten yards driving can be detected. The gear of the car is first made radioactive in a nuclear reactor and then replaced in the car. As the car is driven around a test track, a minute part of the gear wears away and the bits collect in the oil. By measuring the radioactivity of the oil the amount of wear can be determined. Without this technique the car would have to be driven a considerable distance for every measurement and each time the gear would have to be taken out for examination. Many other parts of machines have been tested in this way.

Another nuclear technique enables quantities of impurities as little as one part in ten thousand million to be determined. This is accomplished by neutron activation analysis. A small sample of material is made radioactive in a reactor; the impurity has its own characteristic radiations and the quantity present can be measured. The technique has been used to develop purer materials for transistors, high-strength metal alloys and plastics. It is also used to classify raw materials by their impurity content in industries where such impurities can affect the final product. As vegetation contains trace elements peculiar to the region in which it grows, neutron activation analysis has been used by geologists to locate new ore deposits.

Radioactivity helps to measure
the wear on the gears of cars.

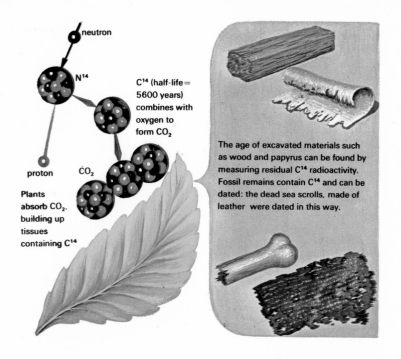

neutron

N¹⁴

proton

CO_2

C^{14} (half-life = 5600 years) combines with oxygen to form CO_2

Plants absorb CO_2, building up tissues containing C^{14}

The age of excavated materials such as wood and papyrus can be found by measuring residual C^{14} radioactivity. Fossil remains contain C^{14} and can be dated: the dead sea scrolls, made of leather were dated in this way.

Carbon-14, produced in the atmosphere by neutrons in cosmic rays colliding with nitrogen atoms, finds its way to all living things.

Carbon Dating

All plants contain carbon-14, and it will be contained in anything made from the plants, such as paper. However, the carbon-14 decays, with a half-life of 5600 years; in 5600 years the paper will have lost half of its radioactivity due to carbon-14. This gives a method of dating old documents by finding the proportion of carbon-14 still present. The measuring equipment has to be carefully shielded from cosmic rays because it has to be extremely sensitive and must measure the weak beta-emission of the material as accurately as possible. The technique has been extremely successful though. It has been used to determine the age of the Dead Sea Scrolls, and also of peat deposits on the sea bed. In the latter case, scientists were able to calculate the date when the vegetation making up the peat was submerged by the rising sea after the last Ice Age.

93

Irradiation Plants

In the applications of radioisotopes so far described, the effect of the radiation on the material being measured or produced has been little, if any. However, with really big sources some materials can be permanently changed.

The most extensive use of gamma radiation is in medical sterilization to kill off bacteria. Syringes, surgical dressings, and many other items are now sterilized and arrive at the doctor's office or the operating room ready for immediate use.

At the irradiation plant the utensils are sealed in small plastic bags and passed on a conveyor system around the source. This usually consists of rods of cobalt-60 assembled in the form of a grid, and the plant is designed to ensure that all the packets get the same dose. The materials themselves are not, of course, made radioactive. The sterilized goods are delivered to the doctor still in their packets and merely have to be removed.

The characteristic blue glow of Cerenkov radiation is caused by a powerful cobalt-60 source submerged in water for storage.

Radiation can, of course, be used to sterilize other materials as well. The first commercial irradiation plant in the world, in Australia, is used to destroy anthrax germs in goat hair used in making carpets.

Food can also be sterilized with gamma rays. In many cases though, it has an unpleasant effect on the taste; however, it is probable that further research will find ways of avoiding this problem. A large-scale plant is already operating in Turkey to disinfect grain. Wheat, barley, rye and corn can be treated at the rate of 30 tons per hour or more. The plant is British designed and operated by the International Atomic Energy Agency.

Radiation is also being used as an alternative to heat, pressure and catalysis as an initiator of chemical reactions. The Dow Chemical Company of Michigan uses gamma rays from cobalt-60 to induce ethylene and hydrogen bromide to react; the plant yields over a million tons of ethyl bromide a year and is operated on a commercial basis. Electron beams can also be used to induce chemicals to react. For instance, they can be used to speed up the curing of paint. The use of these, and of gamma rays, is still in its infancy, but many useful processes may be based on them.

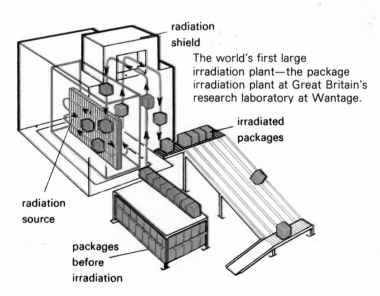

radiation shield

The world's first large irradiation plant—the package irradiation plant at Great Britain's research laboratory at Wantage.

irradiated packages

radiation source

packages before irradiation

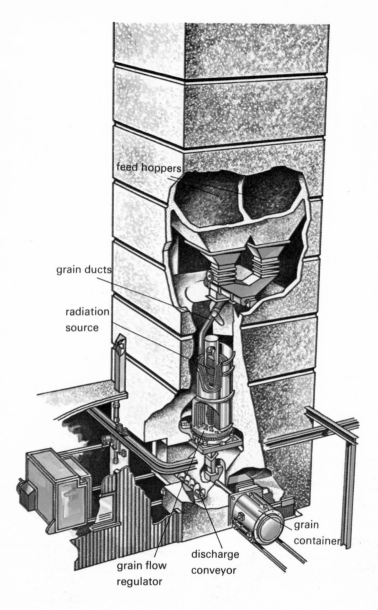

feed hoppers

grain ducts

radiation source

grain flow regulator

discharge conveyor

grain container

The grain irradiation plant at Iskenderun, Turkey uses a massive source of cobalt-60 to prevent breeding of insects in grain and to shorten the lives of existing insects, thereby reducing grain losses.

Power from Radioisotopes

The energy released by radioisotopes as they decay heats up their surroundings. This heat can be converted to electricity, and several isotope-powered devices are producing power for equipment in remote weather stations and for navigational aid and satellites in space.

In these systems the heat is converted to electricity by thermocouples. A thermocouple consists of two conductors made of different metals, joined at both ends, producing a loop in which an electric current will flow when there is a difference in temperature between the two junctions. One junction of each thermocouple is heated by the radioisotope.

A RIPPLE-powered marine light on the Danish coast. The older acetylene lamp, which required regular attention, is situated beside it (left).

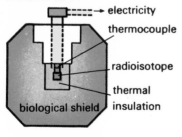

Basic components of a radioisotope generator

Radioisotope power was first conceived for space satellites requiring an electrical power supply of up to 500 watts. The first use in space was in 1961 when a United States satellite carried a supplementary source of electricity for its radio transmitters. Powered by plutonium-238, it produced 2.7 watts. Since then, larger, improved SNAP (Systems for Nuclear Auxiliary Power) units have been developed.

97

The lighthouse at the entrance to Baltimore harbor is powered by 225,000 curies of strontium-90. No lighthouse crew is needed.

These include SNAP-27, for providing power for experiments left on the moon by astronauts.

The first use on earth was the weather station placed on Axel Heiberg Island, Canada, only 700 miles from the North Pole, in 1961. The fuel was strontium-90; this has a suitably long half-life, 28 years, and is readily available from spent nuclear fuel. The success of this 5-watt unit led to other SNAP units, including a 60-watt power supply for a lighthouse at the entrance to Baltimore harbor. Navigational buoys and undersea beacons have also been radioisotope powered.

The British system is designated RIPPLE (Radioisotope Powered Prolonged Life Equipment) and was developed at Harwell. The emphasis has been deliberately placed on the development of low-powered systems of a few watts. One-watt RIPPLEs are operating at the entrance to Stockholm harbor and in Denmark; these power marine navigational lights. Another is operating off Dungeness. A 4-watt RIPPLE powers an aircraft navigational beacon for the airfield on Benbecula, in the Hebrides. All are fueled by strontium-90, in a chemically inert form.

One of the most interesting uses of radioisotopic power will be the nuclear-powered heart pump. In this the radioisotope will power pumps that used to assist or replace the action of a diseased or damaged heart. Plutonium-238, promethium-147 or thulium-171 will be used, and the power will be between 1 and 7 watts. A cardiac 'pacemaker' is also being developed, fueled by plutonium-238. This is not a mechanical heart but a heart-beat stimulator for use in the treatment of heart block or interruption of the normal stimulus of the heart. The device would extend the working life of current models powered by batteries, and is being developed for eventual insertion in the body by surgery.

In all these systems the choice of radioisotope has depended on factors like half-life, the intensity of the radioactivity, and availability. Several radioisotopes of suitable half-life are now easily obtainable, including strontium-90, plutonium-238 and curium-242. Their use is certain to expand: one of the latest applications is a heating system for deep-sea divers.

191427

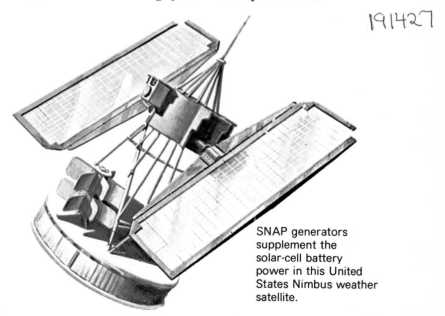

SNAP generators supplement the solar-cell battery power in this United States Nimbus weather satellite.

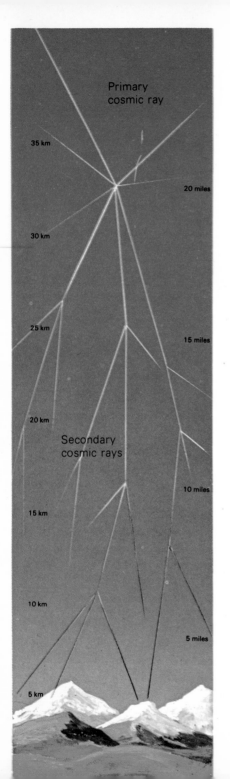

Primary
cosmic ray

35 km

20 miles

30 km

25 km

15 miles

20 km

Secondary
cosmic rays

10 miles

15 km

10 km

5 miles

5 km

LIVING WITH RADIOACTIVITY

Natural Radioactivity

Man has always lived with radioactivity. He has evolved in an environment in which cosmic rays and naturally occurring radioactive materials maintain a continuous background level of radiation.

Cosmic rays—charged particles showering down on earth from outer space—interact with the atoms of the atmosphere, producing radioactive nuclei. The energy of the cosmic rays and the products of their collisions is so great that many reach the earth's surface. Some cosmic rays can even be detected hundreds of feet beneath the earth's surface. A much greater dose is received on a mountain top than at sea level; and the nearer the equator, the smaller the dose.

Cosmic rays are by no means the only radiation reaching earth. To take an obvious éxample, the earth has always been totally dependent on the sun's rays, although most of the ultra-violet radiation is cut off by the atmosphere.

Radioactive material in

A natural radioactive series

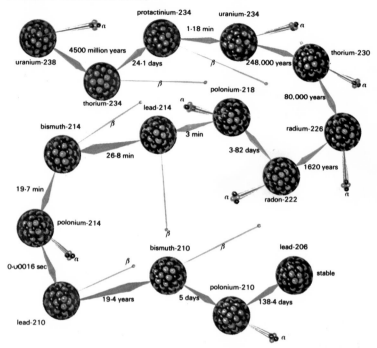

rocks includes uranium-238, thorium-232 and the long list of radioisotopes through which their nuclei decay before they reach a stable form. These constitute the main group of naturally occurring radioisotopes and they are widespread throughout the earth's crust. In parts of Brazil, the thorium mineral monazite occurs in large amounts and raises the background level of radiation considerably. Potassium-40 also occurs fairly widely.

Inevitably, some of this radioactivity is present in food. Carbon-14 occurs in plants. It is produced by the action of cosmic rays on the nitrogen in the atmosphere, and is converted to carbon dioxide, some of which is absorbed by plants; it is then consumed along with the rest of the plant. Radium-226 and thorium-232 also get into food and water. Potassium-40 appears in dairy products and potatoes. Nuts are relatively highly radioactive, particularly Brazil nuts. Inevitably, man himself is slightly radioactive.

Man-Made Radioactivity

During this century, man-made radioactivity has added to natural radiations. Radioisotopes, nuclear reactors, X-ray machines, atom smashers and fallout from nuclear weapons have all been introduced and contribute to the radiation dose.

Medical uses of X-rays account for most of the dose from man-made radiation. Clearly the dose is kept to the minimum and is not in fact dangerous, although the radiographers must take precautions to ensure that they do not receive a large cumulative dose. Workers who regularly use X-rays, such as doctors, dentists or crystallographers, must be especially careful.

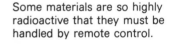

Some materials are so highly radioactive that they must be handled by remote control.

The basic unit of radiation, 1 curie, is produced by 1 gram of radium-226 (half-life 1622 years, *below*). Gold-198 (half-life 2.7 days) is so intensely radioactive that the same amount of radiation is produced by only 0.000004 gram of the isotope (*above*).

It takes 2980 kilograms (about 3 tons) of uranium-238 (half-life 4500 million years) to produce 1 curie of radiation.

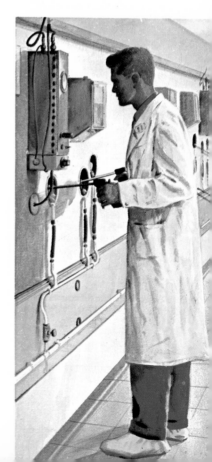

Man-made radioactivity varies from luminous paint on a watch dial to a nuclear explosion. *Left,* the radioactivity symbol.

Some manufactured articles contain natural radioactive materials. The first use for uranium was in glazing china. Radium is used in the luminous paint on the dials of clocks and watches to produce alpha particles that make zinc sulphide in the paint fluoresce. (Radium is being replaced in this trade by tritium, which produces the florescence with beta particles, which are less penetrating.)

A more controversial source of radiation has been the fallout from nuclear weapons. Of the radioisotopes in fallout, strontium-90, caesium-137, iodine-131 and carbon-14 are produced in relatively large amounts, get absorbed by the body and stay there for some time. They get into the body partly by inhalation but mainly in food. The rate of fallout has been highest so far in temperate latitudes of the northern hemisphere, mainly because that is where most nuclear explosions have taken place. However, a careful check is maintained on the dose received. In these latitudes, man-made radiation as a whole accounts, on the average, for only about one-fifth of the individual dose, the rest being from natural sources.

Biological Effects of Radiation

The human body is made up of cells, which, although they vary from tissue to tissue—bone, nerves, muscle, skin—have certain common features. They have a covering membrane, a nucleus containing protein and DNA, and cytoplasm, a semifluid medium surrounding the nucleus and containing the enzymes responsible for the chemical activity of the cell. Radiation may damage any of these but, perhaps most important, it may damage the chromosomes in the cell nucleus.

There are 46 chromosomes in human somatic (or body) cells. During cell division the nucleus and cytoplasm divide into two; each chromosome splits longitudinally into halves, each half going to opposite parts of the cell as the cytoplasm divides.

Sex cells are somewhat different. When formed they each have 23 chromosomes. The total of 46 is re-established when an ovum is fertilized by a spermatozoon. As the chromosomes carry the genes, the complex molecules that determine the patterns of heredity, the resulting embryo has characteristics derived partly from each parent.

Chromosomes can be damaged by ionizing radiations. Broken chromosomes may remain broken or rejoin abnormally, possibly with parts of other chromosomes. Radiation can also alter individual genes, possibly by affecting the complex molecules that form the genes. The overall effect is to interfere with the replication of the chromosomes and to produce mutations.

Mutations occur, of course, spontaneously under normal circumstances. Indeed, the evolution of more and more advanced life forms has come about through spontaneous genetic mutations and natural selection and adaptation to the environment. A great deal of research has been carried out on radiation-induced mutations in mice, rats, rabbits and other animals. Generally, these mutations are similar to those that occur naturally; they can also be produced by certain chemicals. The overall effect of the radiation is merely to increase the numbers of mutations. In practice, radiation has been used to induce mutations in plants, to produce better yields from crops or new varieties of flowers.

Levels of Radioactivity Employed in the Uses of Atomic Energy

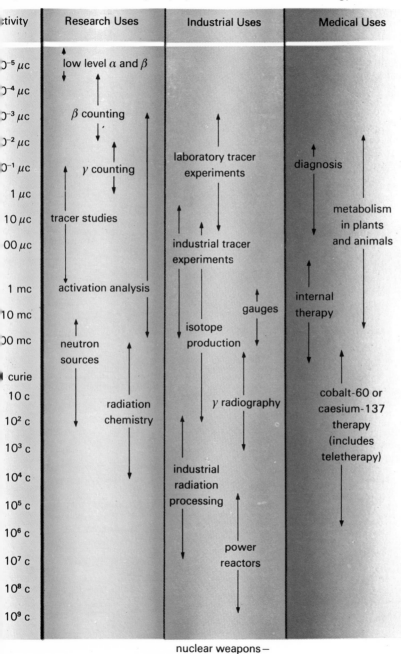

tivity	Research Uses	Industrial Uses	Medical Uses
0^{-5} μc	low level α and β		
0^{-4} μc			
0^{-3} μc	β counting		
0^{-2} μc		laboratory tracer experiments	
0^{-1} μc	γ counting		diagnosis
1 μc			
10 μc	tracer studies		metabolism in plants and animals
00 μc		industrial tracer experiments	
1 mc	activation analysis		internal therapy
10 mc		gauges	
00 mc	neutron sources	isotope production	
curie			
10 c	radiation chemistry	γ radiography	cobalt-60 or caesium-137 therapy (includes teletherapy)
10^2 c			
10^3 c		industrial radiation processing	
10^4 c			
10^5 c			
10^6 c			
10^7 c		power reactors	
10^8 c			
10^9 c			

nuclear weapons — about 10^{14} curies

1 μc = 1 millionth of a curie
1 mc = 1 thousandth of a curie

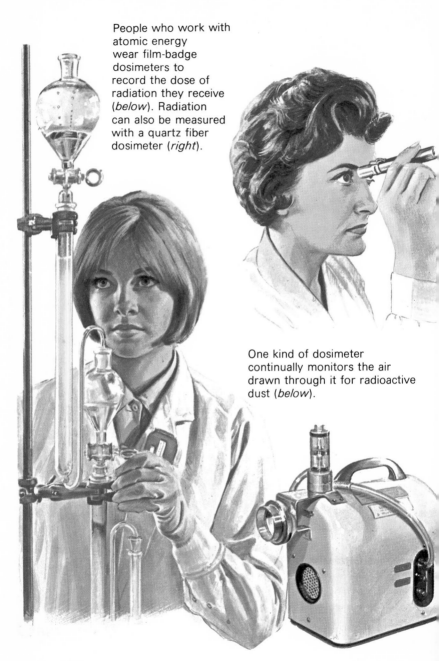

People who work with atomic energy wear film-badge dosimeters to record the dose of radiation they receive (*below*). Radiation can also be measured with a quartz fiber dosimeter (*right*).

One kind of dosimeter continually monitors the air drawn through it for radioactive dust (*below*).

Working with Radiation

The way radiation affects the human being varies, depending upon such factors as the amount, the way it enters the body, the period over which it is received, the type of radiation and the part of the body irradiated. Generally the body can compensate for the damage to human tissue caused by radiation exposure if the damage is not too severe and if it is given time. It is more serious where the total number of the cells of the type damaged is small and they are not replaced by the body. Where the damaged cells are reproductive cells, genetic factors may be involved. The development of atomic energy has made it necessary to ensure that two groups of people are adequately protected—all personnel who use or handle radioactive materials and the public.

One result has been the development of a new profession, that of *health physicist*. His responsibilities include the setting of standards of safe levels of exposure to radiations of different types, the detection of these radiations under various conditions and the development of suitable methods of protection against radiation. Despite the relative newness of this profession it can claim substantial success, which is backed by the virtual absence of radiation accidents.

For the physical monitoring of personnel, both ionization chambers and photographic film are commonly used. Photographic film is usually worn as a badge, about 1½ inches by 2 inches in size. By including two films of different sensitivities it is possible to check the weekly dose (on the more sensitive film) and the dose over a longer period, possibly 13 weeks (on the less sensitive film). The films are wrapped in opaque paper to keep out the light and, in addition, part of the film is covered by a cadmium shield; this absorbs beta particles and only the gamma rays can penetrate it. The unshielded part of the film, accessible to both gamma rays and beta particles, will blacken more and it is possible to distinguish between the dose of each of these radiations received by the individual.

If it is necessary to know the daily dose received by personnel, an ionization chamber is more convenient. As a rule, it resembles a fountain pen and is usually worn clipped inside a pocket. Sometimes a special form of ionization chamber containing a quartz fiber is used; the ionization produced by radiation produces a partial discharge causing the fiber to move across a built-in scale. By holding the dosimeter up to the light and looking through the eyepiece lens, the fiber can be seen against the scale. When the fiber is recharged from a battery it returns to zero on the scale.

Although the unit of radioactivity is the curie, it is usually more important for the health physicist to describe the *radiation dose* (or dose rate) requiring a different unit, the *rad* (for *radiation absorbed dose*). This is defined as the dose of any ionizing radiation which is accompanied by the liberation of 100 ergs of energy per gram of absorbing material. The rad is therefore a useful unit and can be measured with various instruments. However, it is ultimately the biological changes in tissue produced by radiation that are important, and yet another unit is needed to measure the biological effect. This is the *rem* (for *roentgen equivalent man*). One rem is the quantity of any radiation that produces the same biological effect in man as that resulting from the absorption of one rad of X-rays or gamma rays.

Injuries from radiation can be divided into two categories: those from internal radiation and those from external radiation. Internal radiation can be produced by inhaling or swallowing radioactive material or by absorbing it through the skin. Once in the body the radioactive material may eventually bring about various disorders, but radiation from an external source can also produce diseases, such as leukemia.

Methods of protecting personnel against both internal and external radiation have been established. Generally, personnel are protected from high external radiation if the source is surrounded with a material such as lead or concrete. Protection against internal radiation or contamination by radioactive materials is mainly a matter of containing them in suitable structures and of maintaining high standards of general cleanliness within the working area. However, small amounts of radioactive material can be handled with relatively few precautions. On the other hand, some active and toxic materials (such as plutonium) must be completely enclosed, possibly with two layers of protective material.

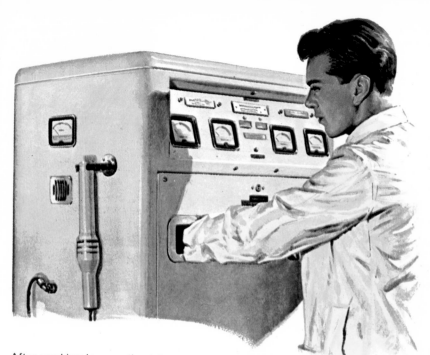

After working in an active laboratory a scientist uses a special monitor to check that there is no contamination left on his hands.

The amount of radioactivity being handled in laboratories has had a considerable effect on their design. Not only is it necessary to protect personnel, it is also necessary to prevent a small quantity of a highly radioactive material from affecting experiments or processes involving slightly active materials. For working with activities below 1 microcurie, ordinary laboratories are generally suitable, with a store for the radioactive materials and a well-shielded room for the counting devices. Greater activities require extra facilities, such as glove boxes and ventilation. Work involving activities above 1 curie is carried out in special 'hot cells' or in cubicles called 'caves' with very thick walls. However, even if there is no shield, the radiation dose is rapidly reduced as the distance from the source increases. Generally, working behind shielding or at a distance from the radiation source means that remote handling methods are required, and many techniques have been developed for this purpose.

Because radioactivity can be transmitted through the air by dust particles, and furthermore can be inhaled, an important

After the technician has been through the shower, he is monitored for radiation.

aspect of the work of the health physicist is the monitoring of the air inside buildings. The air can be drawn through a filter to remove dust particles and the deposits examined. Working areas are monitored with various instruments, some of them fixed, others portable. They include Geiger counters, scintillation counters and ionization chambers. These are also used to monitor actual operations involving the handling of radioactive materials.

A further precaution can be adopted if the radiation level in the working area is still high: the time spent in that area can be strictly limited and the worker can also wear protective clothing. Although this may sometimes consist merely of overalls, for some jobs the worker will wear a plastic suit with its own air supply. This type of clothing is often worn for work inside an active cell, as for some maintenance or decontamination operations. When the worker emerges from the cell he first of all washes and decontaminates his suit under a shower, before taking it off and washing himself. Afterward he is

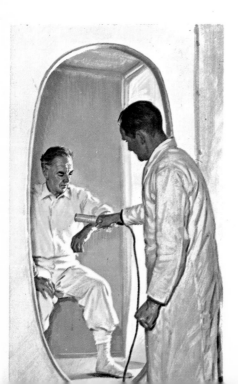

checked for radioactive contamination by automatic monitoring.

In addition to the regular monitoring of personnel, which allows a record to be kept of how much radiation has been received and affords a comparison with the permissible amount, personnel are also kept under regular medical supervision.

Setting the standards of exposure to radiation levels of various kinds has been an important part of health and safety in the atomic energy industry. In the United States the Department of Health has laid down 'minimum permissible levels', and similar organizations have done the same for other countries. The International Commission on Radiological Protection has made recommendations that have been accepted by many countries. These are complex, but they concern the general public as well as personnel in the atomic energy industry.

Protective suits are worn by technicians wherever there is radioactive dust. A supervisor controls clean air supplies to suits.

Why Nuclear Reactors are Safe

Nuclear power stations were usually built in regions of low population; but in various countries, such as Britain and Sweden, plans have now been announced to build reactors in urban areas. Behind this lies the excellent safety record of the nuclear power industry which has helped considerably to dispel early fears.

The safety of nuclear reactors is derived in part at least from certain inherent characteristics. One of these is the 'Doppler Effect'. In general terms, this refers to the fact that, as the temperature of the fuel rises, the proportion of neutrons captured by non-fissioning atoms increases and the rate of fission tends to slow down. It is an automatic and instantaneous effect and immediately resists any increase in the reactor power level. Coupled with other effects, it is a built-in safeguard against the reactor overheating.

The reactor also has as part of its control system devices for automatically shutting down — for example, if there were a 'loss of coolant' or even a partial interruption of coolant flow. Generally, the reactor safety circuits are of extremely conservative design. Quite often they are present in duplicate or triplicate, to ensure reliability.

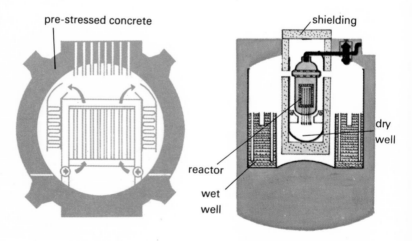

The pre-stressed concrete pressure vessel is a safety feature of the AGR (*left*). The 'pressure suppression' system of containment is used in some reactors (*right*).

The AGR contains shielding to enable operators to work inside parts of the reactor.

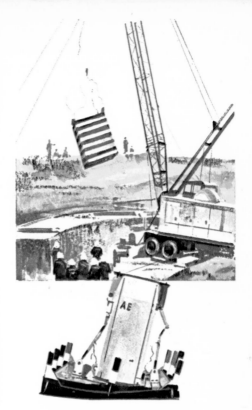

A 9-meter drop test. Only the crate surrounding the lead container is damaged.

Even if there should be an accident in a reactor, the plant is carefully designed to prevent the release of radioactivity to the atmosphere. Not only are fission products normally retained by the fuel and its cladding, there is also around the core the pressure vessel; and in many reactors a further containment system exists.

The advanced gas-cooled reactors are well-known examples of reactors with pre-stressed concrete pressure vessels. These cannot burst suddenly. They form a reliable means of preventing an escape of radioactivity should the reactor coolant become contaminated.

One system operated with some water reactors uses 'pressure suppression'. In this, the entire installation is housed below ground level. The reactor vessel is mounted in a steel containment tank surrounded by a concrete radiation shield. The containment tank, or dry-well, is connected by pipes to a second tank (the 'wet-well'), which is partially filled with water. If there were a vapor release from the reactor, the vapor would pass into the dry-well and then into the wet-well. Not only would the vapor condense, the water in the wet-well would scrub it free of solid radioactive particles.

The emphasis on safety in atomic energy is carried through to the containers for the transport of radioactive material. For instance, the 'type B' containers, which are used to package multi-kilocurie loads of cobalt-60, must be able to survive a 9-meter drop test, a fire test of 800° C for 30 minutes, and a punch test — a drop of 1 meter onto a punch 6 inches in diameter and 9 inches long. Furthermore, as the cobalt-60 gives out heat convection, cooling of the lead container must be allowed during transport. At Albuquerque, in 1965, 10,000 gallons of jet fuel burning for an hour failed to melt a lead pot protected by a special 2-inch shield. -

Containers for radioactive materials must be able to resist fire. In one test, a fire at 1000° C for 1 hour failed to melt a lead pot placed inside a special containment vessel.

Studying the effects of dilute radioactive wastes discharged into the sea includes the examination of marine creatures. The technician (*right*) is taking a blood sample from a lobster.

Radioactive Waste

Radioactive waste is an inevitable by-product of atomic energy. Highly radioactive waste must be stored in such a way that no leakage to the environment can occur, but it is unnecessary to remove completely the activity in low-level wastes, which constitute the main bulk of the waste.

The discharge of radioactive waste from an atomic energy establishment is accompanied by the monitoring of the environment around the site. This is done to find the quantities and composition of the radioactive wastes discharged and to check that their dispersal does not lead to an unacceptable exposure of the public. This latter precaution involves determining not only which radionuclides present the greatest potential danger but also their most likely route into the human body. The most controversial discharges have probably been those into the sea; while the sea is naturally radioactive — one estimate put the total radioactivity content of the oceans at 500 billion curies — the introduction of too much man-made radioactivity might have very harmful effects for all kinds of life.

THERMONUCLEAR FUSION

Fusion Reactions

It was explained in the first chapter that energy is produced in fission reactions because matter is converted to energy when uranium-235 atoms are split. A similar conversion occurs when light atoms such as hydrogen and deuterium fuse, or join together to build heavier atoms.

Fusion reactions are the source of energy in the greatest power-producers of all—the stars. Although a star begins as a cloud of hydrogen gas, contraction, caused by its own gravitational attraction, increases its pressure, density, and temperature. The collisions between atoms increase in number and violence until eventually they strip away electrons. The mass of nuclei and electrons produced is known as a *plasma*. It is the fourth state of matter (the other three being solid, liquid and gas). It is in plasma that the fusion reactions take place.

Fusion reactions are also the basis of the hydrogen bomb. It would be impossible to slow down an H-bomb and release the energy in a controlled manner because it would need a fission bomb to detonate it.

Today world-wide attention is focused on the possibility of producing controlled thermonuclear reactions by simulating

A solar flare. The sun derives energy from fusion reactions.

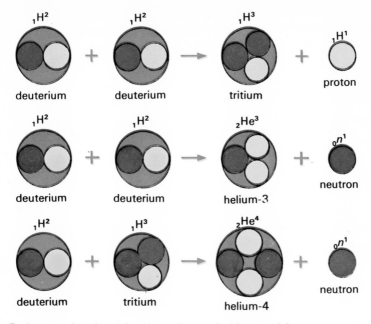

Fusion reactions involving deuterium and tritium nuclei.

the conditions in the sun and stars, that is, with a very hot plasma. This involves heating a gas until it becomes a plasma, then heating it further while containing it in some way. For fusion to be an economical source of power, enough energy would have to be released in the reaction to exceed the sum of the energy needed to heat the gas and the energy lost from the plasma as radiation. However fusion is still at an experimental stage and it will be decades before electricity is produced by this means. Nevertheless, the prospect is an enticing one, if only because of the abundance of deuterium — 1 pound of deuterium can release energy equivalent to 3,000,000 pounds of coal.

To maximize the number of energy-producing collisions, the greatest possible number of nuclei must be held together at the highest possible temperature for as long as possible. The sort of temperature needed for deuterium nuclei to fuse is 300,000,000°C, with 10^{15} nuclei contained for 10 seconds. This density of ions (10^{15}) is not hard to achieve, since it is only about a ten-thousandth of the density of the atmosphere. But although various ways of heating the plasma exist, none of them raises it to a high enough temperature for durations longer than a few thousandths of a second.

Even if a plasma at 300,000,000° C could be achieved, it would still have to have a container. Providing the container is a fundamental problem. Loss of energy to the walls of the vessel lowers the temperature of the plasma. The methods being studied are based on the use of strong magnetic fields and often involve considerable ingenuity.

The particles in a plasma will normally be moving in random directions at thousands of miles a second. But they are all charged and will all be affected by a magnetic field. In fact, if a uniform magnetic field is applied to the plasma the particles will move in spiral paths, each encircling a line of force. Positively charged particles spiral in one direction, negative particles in the other. Unless they collide, the particles do not move across the lines of force and therefore cannot easily reach the walls of the container.

Particles will drift, however, if the magnetic field is not uniform; the stronger

With no magnetic field, plasma particles move randomly.

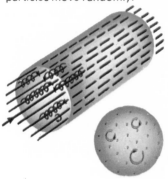

Plasma particles in a uniform magnetic field

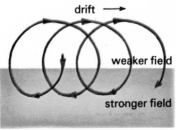

Plasma particles in a non-uniform magnetic field

The pinch effect

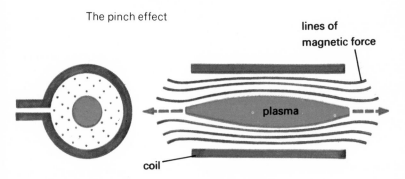

lines of
magnetic force

plasma

coil

A simple open-ended straight-tube magnetic trap

the field, the smaller the radius of curvature of the spiral path, so that as a particle moves in and out of the stronger region it also moves sideways. This tends to make the whole plasma drift, but provided a uniform field is produced, it should be possible to contain the extremely hot gas.

In one type of containment the ends of the plasma are joined up to form a doughnut-shaped torus. Zeta (zero energy thermonuclear apparatus), a British fusion experiment, uses this system. It produces a magnetic field by passing a current through the plasma; the magnetic field compresses—or pinches—the plasma and also heats it up. The name 'pinch effect' is commonly applied to this type of containment. In other toroidal systems, a strong axial magnetic field is applied around the outside of the plasma by a coil of wire wound around the torus; this is used in the 'stellarator' system. Other types of containment use straight tubes and complex magnetic fields to minimize plasma losses in the system.

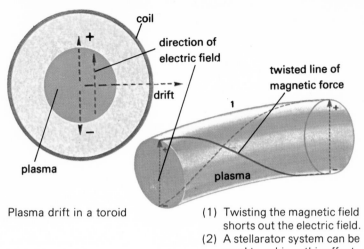

Plasma drift in a toroid

(1) Twisting the magnetic field shorts out the electric field.
(2) A stellarator system can be used to achieve this effect.

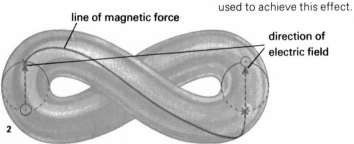

Toroidal Systems

The toroidal shape, despite its apparent simplicity, has one inherent disadvantage: the magnetic field is stronger on the inside because it is 'bunched up'. A non-uniform magnetic field tends to split up the plasma into its two components, ions and electrons. These move in opposite directions. As they part, they produce an electric field in the plasma perpendicular to the toroidal magnetic field, which pushes both ions and electrons toward the outer wall of the container. One way of preventing this plasma drift is to short out the electric fields producing the drift. This can be done by twisting the magnetic field so that the lines of force pass through opposite polarities of the electric fields; particles spiraling along them will cancel out the fields. The stellarator system, developed at Princeton University, originally achieved this by twisting the entire torus into a figure-eight. However, it was realized that the same effect could be achieved with two sets of magnetic field coils.

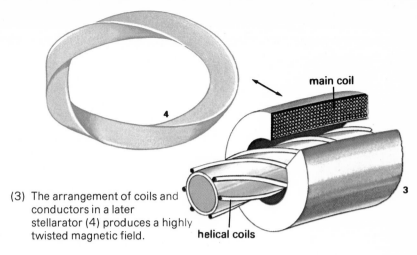

(3) The arrangement of coils and conductors in a later stellarator (4) produces a highly twisted magnetic field.

main coil

helical coils

(5) Shear in zeta.

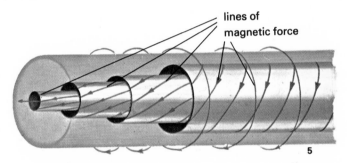

lines of magnetic force

One set — the confining coils — produces the axial field, and the other — the helical windings — provides the required twist.

In zeta the twist in the lines of force is produced by combining a toroidal field with the field producing the pinch. The lines of force at the center are straight and those at the outside of the plasma are circular; in between, within the plasma, there is continuous transition — the lines of force are helices, each with a different pitch. The effect is one of shear in the plasma, improving its stability as well as producing plasma drift. However, there is one other force in zeta tending to drive the plasma to the walls of the container; the plasma ring tends to expand. To correct this, the torus is surrounded by a highly conducting metal wall. The magnetic field is squashed by the expanding ring against the wall but cannot pierce it; a restoring force is set up which opposes the expansion of the ring.

Maintaining the plasma in an equilibrium position is not the only problem encountered in toroidal containers. Various instabilities can appear within the plasma. For instance, if a small bend occurs in the plasma the concentration of magnetic field on the inside makes the kink grow worse, until the plasma touches the container wall or breaks up entirely. Similarly, if a small constriction appears in the plasma, the concentration of the magnetic field in the constricted region will squeeze the plasma even more and thus it quickly breaks apart.

Instabilities such as these have prevented the pinch effect from becoming any more than a momentary phenomenon. The study of instabilities is therefore a feature of fusion research. They fall into two broad categories, macroinstabilities and microinstabilities. The macroinstabilities are often called magnetohydrodynamic (MHD) instabilities. They have been studied in detail in several experiments.

The kink and constriction instabilities are of this type, in particular the group known as 'interchange instabilities'. Interchange instabilities in toroids are canceled out by the measures needed in any case to prevent plasma drift. The shear in the

Zeta (zero energy thermonuclear apparatus), a fusion experiment at the Culham laboratory in Great Britain.

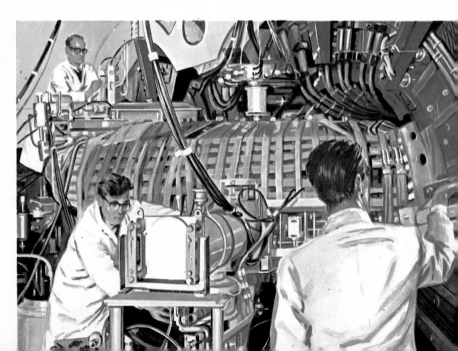

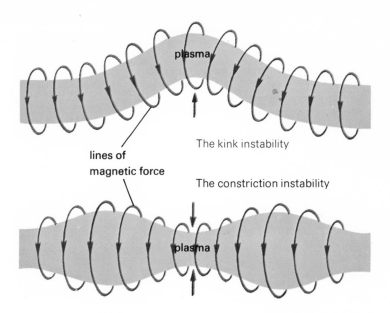

plasma

The kink instability

lines of
magnetic force

The constriction instability

plasma

plasma in zeta is effective in this way. With this equipment, which is, it must be emphasized, an experiment and not a reactor, temperatures of over a million degrees have been obtained with a containment figure (n, the number of nuclei per cc., multiplied by t, the time for which it is contained in seconds) of 10^{11}. This is, of course, much less than the goal for both temperature and containment figure.

An improved toroidal system, in which the shear is considerably strengthened, has been developed, called the *hard core*, or *inverted, pinch*. In this, the two magnetic fields are swopped over: the concentric one is on the inside and the axial one is on the outside. The inner, concentric field is produced by a rod, through the middle of the discharge tube, connected to an electrode; external coils supply the axial field. The current flows along the center rod and returns, partly through the plasma and partly through the outer wall. The concentric field around the rod pushes the plasma against the surrounding axial field. Even in this system instabilities occur, mainly because the plasma is not a perfect conductor. Studies of toroidal systems are continuing in many parts of the world.

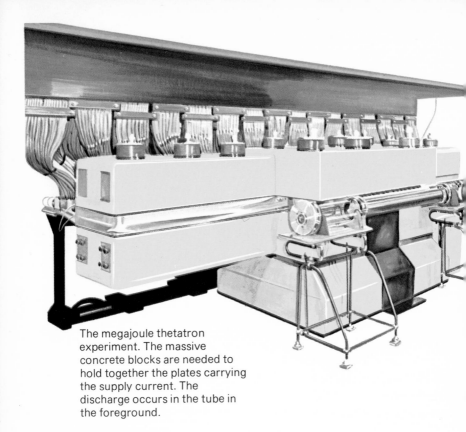

The megajoule thetatron experiment. The massive concrete blocks are needed to hold together the plates carrying the supply current. The discharge occurs in the tube in the foreground.

Magnetic Bottles

Basically, a magnetic bottle consists of a coil surrounding a straight tube (possibly made of quartz) containing a plasma. The plasma can be formed by passing a strong electric current along the axis of the tube, through deuterium gas. To compress the plasma and raise its temperature, the coil is energized. This is the basis of a type of magnetic trap called the thetatron. The Culham laboratory's megajoule thetatron can heat a plasma with a density of 10^{16} nuclei per cc. to about $1,000,000°$ C and contain it for a few millionths of a second. The compressed plasma flows out of the ends of the trap, and this leak determines the containment time.

Despite the extreme shortness of the containment time, the plasma might be expected to be stable. But in practice it is not, and the thetatron plays an important part in the study of this interchange instability, one of the most important instabilities of magnetically confined plasmas.

The inverted
beaker analogy of
interchange
instability (*right*)

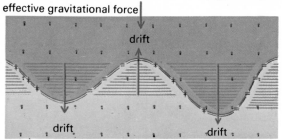

Ripples in a plasma boundary (*below*). The red dots indicate lines of magnetic force.

effective gravitational force

drift

drift

drift

This instability is best understood by analogy with an inverted beaker in which water is supported by a leakproof and frictionless piston; the water would be supported only by the pressure of the air. If the piston were removed, a small ripple might initially develop. It would then grow, because less water is pushing down on the trough than on the crest, and the water would soon fall out of the beaker. Similarly, a ripple at the boundary between a column of plasma and the surrounding vacuum—caused possibly by the bumps in the plasma—will tend to grow under the influence of a gravitational-like force. Within the bump, the nuclei and electrons will drift in opposite directions. This produces an electric field, transverse to both the magnetic and the 'gravitational' field, that makes the nuclei and electrons—in fact, the entire bump—drift downward, and enlarges the ripple. In the thetatron, the force equivalent to the 'gravitational' force is produced because the plasma column spins.

A magnetic bottle much more stable against interchange instabilities is that based on cusp geometry. The convex curvature of the magnetic field toward the plasma produces stability because the magnetic field strength increases in all

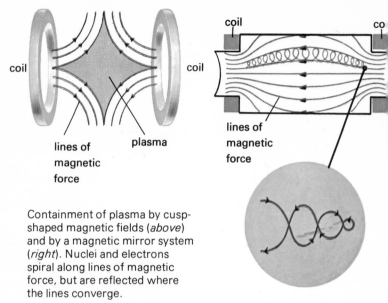

coil

coil

coil

co

lines of
magnetic
force

plasma

lines of
magnetic
force

Containment of plasma by cusp-
shaped magnetic fields (*above*)
and by a magnetic mirror system
(*right*). Nuclei and electrons
spiral along lines of magnetic
force, but are reflected where
the lines converge.

directions away from the center of the plasma, where it is zero.
The plasma can be considered to be at the bottom of a three-
dimensional magnetic well.

The plasma is produced in the cusp by firing two blobs of hot
dense plasma into the evacuated vessel from either end. As the
blobs meet at the center, the cusp fields are rapidly established
around them, compressing and heating the plasma. Temperatures of about 1,000,000° C have to be produced. A cusp magnetic bottle has more leaks than a thetatron: it has a leak all
around the middle as well as at the two ends. But experiments
have shown that, although the plasma exists only for a few
thousandths of a second, it is free from interchange instabilities.

One other important class of magnetic bottle is the magnetic
mirror system. This uses a low-density plasma permeated with
a magnetic field. The nuclei and electrons can move considerable distances between collisions. At each end of the tube the
magnetic field lines are made to converge. As the plasma particles approach each end they are forced to increase their rota-
tional energy at the expense of their forward motion, and eventually they reverse their direction; the ions are reflected, as if
by a magnetic mirror.

Two interesting magnetic mirror systems are in use at the Culham laboratory in Great Britain. In the first of these, used in the magnetic trap stability experiment (MTSE), a burst of hot plasma from a plasma gun is guided through a conveying magnetic field into a region where the field strength is initially uniform. Extra field coils are rapidly energized, first ahead of the plasma and then behind it. A large proportion of the plasma is then reflected to and fro between the magnetic mirrors.

If ions are injected into a plasma they are immediately ejected. Therefore, in the second system, Phoenix I, neutral particles formed by neutralizing an accelerated beam of ions are passed into the magnetic trap shortly after they are produced; for a brief period the electrons are so loosely attached to the nuclei that they can be stripped away by the forces acting on the particles as they traverse the magnetic field. The ions and electrons produced spiral round magnetic field lines and are reflected between magnetic mirrors.

Injecting plasma into a magnetic mirror system. Coil M2 is energized and produces a magnetic mirror. The plasma is reflected but is trapped because another magnetic mirror has been formed behind it by M1.

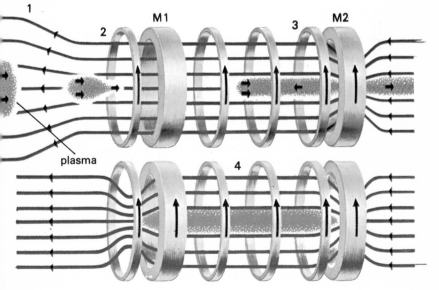

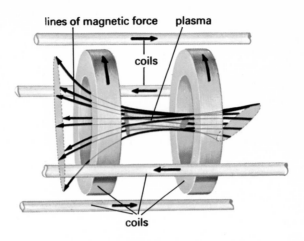

Cusp geometry combined with a magnetic mirror system

Elegant though these systems are, the plasma is still unstable. In Phoenix I, for instance, interchange instabilities quickly deform the plasma. However, this can be remedied by transforming the trap into a magnetic well, that is, by making the magnetic field intensity increase in all directions away from the center of the plasma. This already happens toward each magnetic mirror, so it is merely necessary to add magnetic fields that increase radially away from the axis of the trap. The result is a combination of mirror system (which is a good container) and cusp geometry (which has good stability).

Another experiment at the Culham laboratory, Phoenix II, achieves this with four extra field coils and the mirror system. All the field lines lead away from the center of the plasma, which has a diameter of roughly six inches. This type of containment has shown good stability against large-scale magnetohydrodynamic instablilities.

An unusual concept has been developed in the United States: the 'astron'. This produces a toroidal magnetic field within an open-ended tube. It has already been claimed that this system has produced a 5 percent magnetic bottle. The astron is situated at the Lawrence Radiation Laboratory, Livermore, which is building a new accelerator with which it is hoped to raise the system to a 100 percent magnetic bottle.

The experiments described show considerable progress in overcoming the problem of containing the plasma and the large-scale instabilities; the instabilities are suppressed either by magnetic wells or by the use of sheared magnetic fields. There remains the microinstabilities.

Microinstabilities are caused by the build-up of waves, pulsations or other small disturbances in the plasma. Ordinary fluids have similar disturbances—for instance, the turbulent flow of a liquid in a pipe. Unfortunately, unlike the liquid, a plasma is not a simple fluid but should be regarded as a mixture of two gases, one positive and one negative. The disturbances are accentuated by the electrical charges and can become so violent that they cause complete break-up of the plasma.

Experiments are in progress in many countries to investigate the way these instabilities grow and propagate, and to study the basic physics of plasma. Despite the difficulties, it is expected, if only because of the genuine international cooperation in this field, that progress will be steady.

Plasma in a magnetic well. Here the magnetic field lines produced by combining cusp and magnetic mirror systems and then simplifying the system are shown on the surface on the plasma.

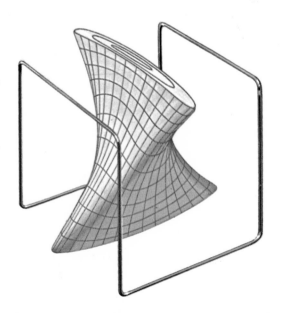

Technicians building a small torus experiment

Fusion Technology

In the study of fusion, many of the experiments present technological and engineering problems often far removed from conventional practice. For instance, in one pinch experiment the basic requirement is to maintain an electric field of 1000 volts per centimeter along the length of a preheated plasma for about a millionth of a second. To accomplish this, 40 capacitors, storing a total of 100 kilojoules of energy when charged to 100 kilovolts, are connected in parallel to the load through 40 special switches and cables. All 40 switches must be fired within two hundred millionths of a second.

In other experiments with magnetic traps the magnetic fields required are huge, demanding powerful current supplies for the electromagnets. To reduce this need for such enormous currents, components relying on super-conductivity have been developed. In these the coils are cooled to near absolute zero, where their electrical resistance is very small.

A magnetically confined high-temperature plasma releases radiation, nuclei and electrons that bombard the walls of the container. This can release large quantities of gas, which can enter the plasma and cool it. One of the advancing fields of fusion technology is in the maintenance of the vacuum around the plasma.

A basic need in any scientific research is the need to make measurements. This is particularly difficult in fusion research, but a number of techniques have been developed under the general name of 'plasma diagnostics'. The quantities commonly measured are the plasma current, the electron density, the energy and temperature of the ions and electrons, the distribution of the magnetic field and the neutron emission (the number and energy of the neutrons emitted in the fusion reaction is an indication of the extent of the reaction). The basic difficulty is the transient and fluctuating nature of the plasma and the multiplicity of phenomena. Generally, several methods are used independently for making a particular measurement.

Instruments used for studying the plasma

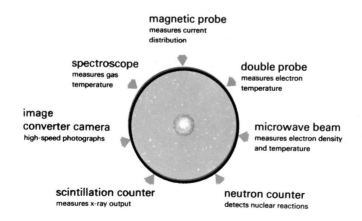

magnetic probe
measures current
distribution

spectroscope
measures gas
temperature

double probe
measures electron
temperature

**image
converter camera**
high-speed photographs

microwave beam
measures electron density
and temperature

scintillation counter
measures x-ray output

neutron counter
detects nuclear reactions

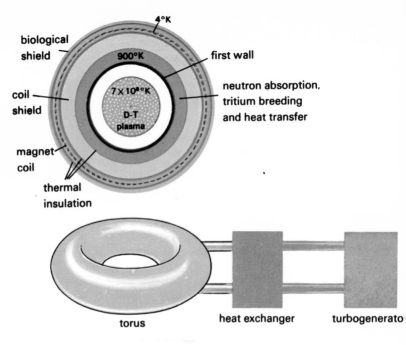

The basic components of a fusion power station (based on a concept by W. G. Holmeyer, Massachusetts Institute of Technology)

A Fusion Power Station

Despite the problems facing fusion scientists and technologists, it is possible to estimate just what a fusion power station should look like. As we have already seen, the plasma must be contained magnetically, probably in a torus. The wall of the torus must satisfy certain requirements for mechanical strength, heat transfer and nuclear properties. There must be a coolant to circulate around this wall. Outside this there should be a 'blanket' in which tritium fuel can be bred from the light isotope of lithium, because tritium is not available from natural sources.

The toroidal structure would be about 50 feet in diameter and have an output of 5,000,000 kilowatts of heat. The coolant would be passed through heat exchangers to produce steam for a turbogenerator.

PARTICLE ACCELERATORS

In 1935, the Japanese scientist H. Yukawa predicted the existance of a particle which became known as the pi-meson (or pion). He predicted it on theoretical grounds, to account for the 'nuclear glue' that holds the nucleus together. In 1947 such a particle was identified in cosmic radiation. According to theory, it is the exchange of pi-mesons between neutrons and protons in the nucleus that binds the nucleus.

In addition to the pi-meson many other elementary particles have been discovered in recent years. Many early discoveries were made by studying cosmic ray interactions. Then machines were developed to accelerate particles to higher and higher energies and to make them interact with matter, producing new particles. The energy of accelerated particles is measured in electron volts (eV); one electron volt is the energy given to an electron when it is pushed by an electrical force due to a potential difference of one volt. The biggest accelerators push their particles to energies of thousands of millions of electron volts.

Particle accelerators enable the interaction of particles to be studied in the laboratory, under controlled conditions. They can accelerate electrons, protons, deuterons (deuterium nuclei), alpha particles or even larger fragments of atoms, and direct them at a target made of suitable material. The nuclear reactions produced by the collisions are then followed by instruments which detect the products of the reactions.

The 'nuclear glue' which holds the nucleus together is provided by the exchange of pi-mesons by nucleons such as protons.

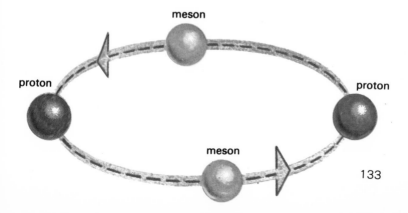

Early Particle Accelerators

The splitting of the atom by J. D. Cockroft and E. T. S. Walton, performed at the Cavendish Laboratory, Cambridge, England in 1931, was among the first nuclear experiments with an accelerator. They accelerated protons to 700,000 eV by discharging a bank of condensers charged to 10,000 volts. The protons bombarded lithium-7 isotope in lithium oxide, producing alpha particles (helium nuclei):

$$\underset{\text{proton}}{{}^{7}_{3}\text{Li} + {}^{1}_{1}\text{H}} \rightarrow \underset{\text{alpha particles}}{{}^{4}_{2}\text{He} + {}^{4}_{2}\text{He}}$$

Nuclear experiments had previously been carried out with 'natural' particles, such as the fast-moving alpha particles used by Ernest Rutherford in 1919 when he achieved the first artificial transmutation of atoms:

$$\underset{\text{nitrogen}}{{}^{14}_{7}\text{N}} + \underset{\text{alpha particle}}{{}^{4}_{2}\text{He}} \rightarrow \underset{\text{proton}}{{}^{1}_{1}\text{H}} + \underset{\text{oxygen}}{{}^{17}_{8}\text{O}}$$

These alpha particles were obtained by radioactive decay. Cockroft and Walton's achievement was to use artificially accelerated particles.

The accelerator with which Cockroft and Walton split the atom.

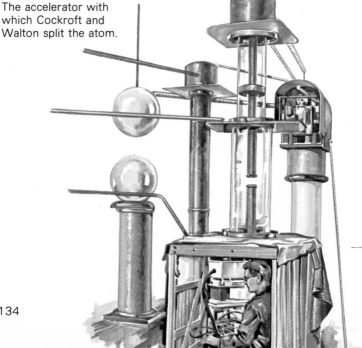

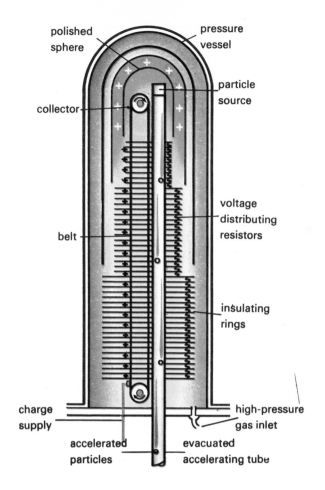

polished sphere

pressure vessel

particle source

collector

voltage distributing resistors

belt

insulating rings

charge supply

high-pressure gas inlet

accelerated particles

evacuated accelerating tube

The Van der Graaff accelerator contains a hollow sphere that can build up a very high electric potential. A belt made of non-conducting material is sprayed with electric charge at the base of the machine. The belt is driven at high speed and the charge collected from it at the top and conducted to the sphere. When the sphere attains a maximum potential, protons or other particles are ejected from the particle source and accelerated by the large potential difference between the sphere and the base of the machine. By using several accelerators in series, protons with energies of 20 MeV or more can be produced.

Another machine designed and developed by Robert Van de Graaff in the early 1930's is shown above.

Cyclotrons

Other ways of achieving high energies were being investigated when Van de Graaff and Cockroft and Walton were building their machines. One somewhat different approach was to use a series of successive small accelerations to achieve the effect of the one-stage acceleration. This was the basis of the cyclotron, invented by E. O. Lawrence at the University of California in 1929. Because cyclotrons are used to make radioisotopes, the principle of the cyclotron is described in detail on page 77.

There is a limit to the particle energy attainable with a cyclotron. According to relativity theory, the mass of a particle increases as its energy increases. Thus, as the velocity of the particle approaches the velocity of light the increase in mass becomes great. When the mass of the accelerating proton in a fixed-frequency cyclotron becomes very large, it no longer gains enough additional speed in each half orbit to make up for the fact that it is traveling in a wider arc. It will reach the gap between the dees too late to receive a push from the alternating voltage; the electric field will be against it and it will be slowed down.

A beam of deuterons shown emerging from a cyclotron (at the Argonne National Laboratory in America) is 'visible' because the deuterons are exciting air molecules along their path.

This theoretical limit is surmounted in modern cyclotrons. In one type, the isochronous cyclotron, the magnetic field is increased in the outer regions to compensate for the relativistic increase in mass of the accelerated particles. About twenty cyclotrons of this type are in operation throughout the world.

In yet another version of the cyclotron, it is the frequency of the alternating current that is varied, decreasing to match the lower rate of revolution of the particles. This is the synchrocyclotron. This type of machine accelerates protons in bursts, pushing one group through an entire cycle before beginning to accelerate a new group. The number of complete cycles is an important characteristic of a synchrocyclotron—with some machines there can be as many as 300 per second.

The 740-MeV synchrocyclotron at Berkeley, California, was the first accelerator used to create artificial pi-mesons, and at CERN (the European Center for Nuclear Research, near Geneva, Switzerland), the decay of a pi-meson into an electron and a neutral particle of no mass called the neutrino was first observed at the 600-MeV synchrocyclotron.

The variable energy cyclotron at Harwell in Great Britain is used by chemists and metallurgists. After particles leave the cyclotron they travel down evacuated pipes, through bending and focusing magnets into three 'target rooms' where apparatus is set up.

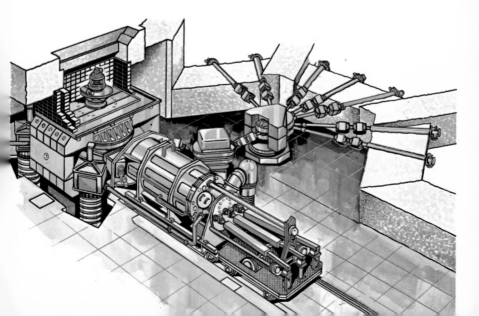

Synchrotrons

Synchrocyclotrons are big, and the magnet in particular is expensive. Consequently, although there is no theoretical limit to the particle energy achievable, there is a practical limit due to the cost of the magnet. For this reason, a technique somewhat different from that of the synchrocyclotron has been developed to accelerate protons to energies in the BeV range (a thousand million or billion electron volts, B standing for billion).

The protons must usually first be accelerated to an energy of about 6 to 10 MeV (millions of electron volts) by a Van de Graaff electrostatic generator or a linear accelerator. The protons are then forced into a near constant circular path by means of a ring-shaped magnet system surrounding a tube containing the particles. To keep the particles moving in a path of almost constant radius in spite of their increasing energy and momentum, the magnetic field is increased correspondingly. As in the synchrocyclotron the frequency of the oscillating potential is also increased to keep the particles in phase with the oscillations. Accelerators of this type are called proton synchrotrons, and have been constructed in the United States, Great Britain,

In the Bevatron, a 6.2 BeV proton synchrotron at Berkeley, California, protons already energized make three or four million revolutions before leaving the machine at 99 percent of the speed of light. The resulting reactions are detected in the cloud chamber.

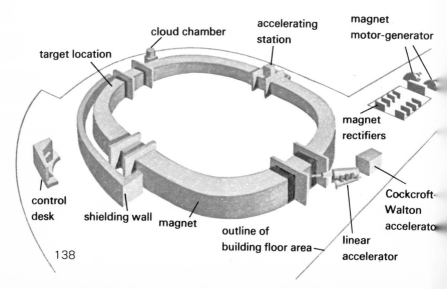

138

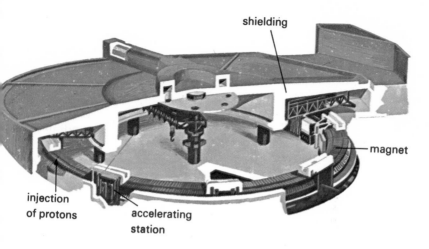

Nimrod, a 7 BeV proton synchrotron at Harwell in Great Britain

France, the Netherlands and the Soviet Union.

The most obvious feature of a proton synchrotron is the magnet. The size of this is decided partly by the energy of the machine, which determines its diameter, and partly by the way the particles are concentrated in the magnetic field—oscillation of the beam around the orbit can be reduced by 'strong focusing', and the vacuum tank in which it travels can be made smaller and the magnet size reduced.

Strong focusing is used in the more powerful proton synchrotrons. These are the 33 BeV alternation gradient synchrotron at the Brookhaven National Laboratory, in Mississippi, the 30 BeV machine at CERN, and the 70 BeV machine at Serpukhov, in Russia.

A machine of 200 BeV is to be built in the United States, near Weston, Illinois. In this machine the protons will be accelerated in four stages; the last stage will be seven-eighths of a mile in diameter and the mass of the magnet will be 19,400 tons. CERN has designed a 300 BeV proton synchrotron for construction somewhere in Europe, but it depends upon international agreement for the financing of the project. Ultimately, a machine capable of thousands of BeVs may be built, but this would probably require cooperative effort on the part of a number of countries.

Electron Accelerators

Certain machines have been especially developed to accelerate electrons to high energies. The betatron, for instance, can be used to accelerate electrons to 300 MeV. A betatron works in a similar way to a transformer. That is, an alternating current applied to a primary coil induces a similar, secondary current (flow of electrons) in what in a transformer would be the secondary coil, but in the betatron is a ring-shaped evacuated glass tube placed between the poles of a magnet. The secondary current is produced because the primary current energizes the electromagnet. As the magnetic field builds up, electrons, produced from a heated filament, are accelerated around the evacuated tube. The magnetic field keeps them moving in a curved path until they reach a maximum energy, at which point they are ejected from the machine. During this time the electrons make many tens of thousands of revolutions in the evacuated tube and, in the biggest betatrons, may attain 99.99 percent of the speed of light.

The first betatron was built by D. W. Kerst in 1940 at the University of Illinois; it accelerated electrons to 2.3 MeV. Now the same university has another machine, the most powerful betatron in the world. It accelerates electrons to 340 MeV.

Synchrotrons have been developed to accelerate electrons as well as protons. The technique is basically the same as for

In the betatron, the current in the primary windings energizes the magnet and as the magnetic field builds up, electrons are accelerated in the tube between the poles of the magnet.

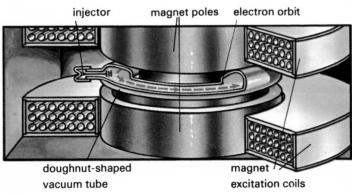

injector   magnet poles   electron orbit

doughnut-shaped   magnet
vacuum tube   excitation coils

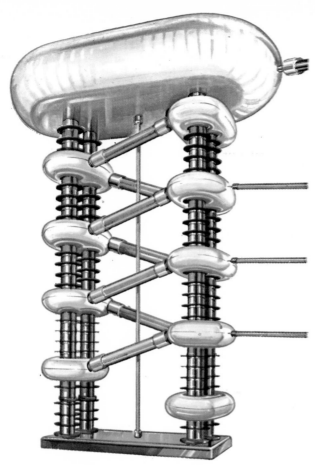

A modern Cockroft-Walton
machine in the injector room of
the 50 MeV proton linear
accelerator at the Rutherford
High Energy Laboratory, at
Harwell in Great Britain.

protons, with a betatron providing the initial acceleration.
Generally, electron synchrotrons do not operate at the energy
levels of proton synchrotrons, but for a given energy electrons
travel 2,000 times as fast as protons. Machines such as the 4
BeV electron synchrotron at Daresbury, Cheshire, in Great
Britain, are powerful tools for probing the structure of protons
and neutrons.

Linear Accelerators

One important class of accelerator avoids the need for giant magnets—the linear accelerator. In its earliest form, it consisted of a series of electrodes with alternate electrodes linked together. Adjacent electrodes carried opposite charges, which reversed with each half-cycle of the applied electric field. Holes bored through the electrodes permitted the passage of an ion beam that was accelerated by the potential difference between successive adjacent electrodes. To keep the beam in time with the oscillating voltage, the electrodes were designed in successively increasing length.

Newer versions have been developed, based on microwave technology. A two-mile long machine has been built at Stanford University, California. It can accelerate electrons to 20

Fragments of heavy nuclei can be hurled along this ion linear accelerator at the Lawrence Radiation Laboratory, in the University of California, to reach an energy of 10 MeV.

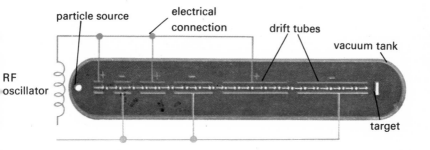

particle source

electrical connection

drift tubes

vacuum tank

RF oscillator

target

A linear accelerator

BeV and may eventually be modified to achieve twice this figure. 'Linacs', as they are called, are particularly useful for accelerating electrons because they avoid the radiation loss that occurs when electrons are accelerated in a synchrotron.

A proton linear accelerator has been used for some years at the Rutherford High Energy Laboratory. This 50 MeV machine is employed in experiments on proton scattering and proton-induced nuclear reactions.

Linear accelerators are widely used as pre-acceleration stages for large synchrotrons. They are also used to accelerate heavy ions such as lithium, carbon, neon and argon.

However, the ultimate in heavy ion accelerators, already named the Omnitron because it will accelerate the ions of any element (even those heavier than uranium), will use a synchrotron.

Storage Rings

An interesting innovation in the drive to higher energies and beam intensities is the use of storage rings to bring about collisions between energetic particles traveling in opposite directions. The energy involved in the collision is the sum of the energies of each of the particles. Illustrations show two systems now in use. The storage rings are basically doughnut-shaped tubes surrounded by magnets to give a magnetic field strong enough to keep energetic particles circulating at constant radius for an appreciable time. A large particle density can be built up in the storage ring by injecting a number of pulses from the accelerator, a procedure known as beam stacking.

Storage rings are in use or under construction for a number of studies. Two-ring storage systems like that shown for electron-electron collisions have been used in the United States and the Soviet Union. For studies of electron-positron collisions the system is simpler because these particles will circulate in opposite directions in the same magnetic field, and a single storage ring can be used. Collisions between 1.5 BeV positrons and electrons have been studied at Frascati, Italy. Proton-proton collisions will be investigated at CERN by circulating two beams in opposite directions in a single storage ring. Two sets of magnets will be used. About 400 pulses of high-energy

The CERN muon storage ring. Half of the ring is surrounded by concrete shielding.

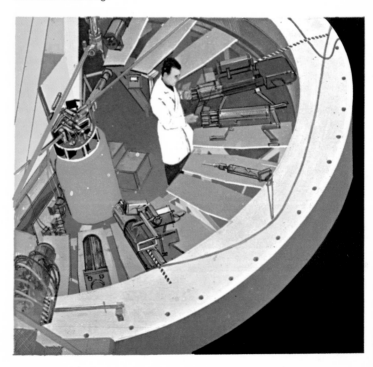

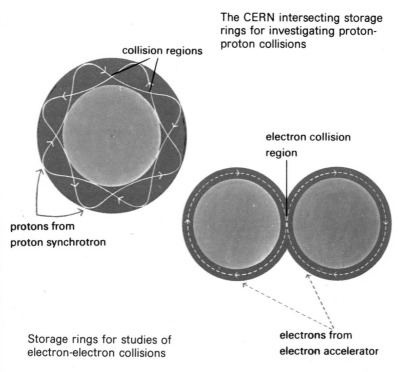

The CERN intersecting storage rings for investigating proton-proton collisions

collision regions

electron collision region

protons from proton synchrotron

Storage rings for studies of electron-electron collisions

electrons from electron accelerator

protons will be injected into the 1000-foot-diameter storage ring and stacked with one set of magnets operating. Then protons will be injected in the opposite direction with the other set of magnets energized. The paths of the two beams are distorted by the two sets of magnets so that they intersect in eight places. The rings are scheduled to be in operation in 1971. Proton-antiproton collisions are to be investigated in a facility being built at the Nuclear Physics Institute at Novosibirsk, in Russia. A pulse of 25 BeV protons striking a target will produce antiprotons that will be stored in a subsidiary ring until more than 10 billion antiprotons are present. The antiprotons will then be returned to the accelerator ring where they will collide with high energy protons traveling in the opposite direction.

Storage rings are unquestionably valuable additions to the equipment of the nuclear physicist. However, they are built for the purpose of studying specific reactions and do not have the flexibility of modern accelerators.

Particle Detectors

An important part of nuclear physics is the equipment used for detecting the reactions. Scintillation counters can be used on the particle tracks which are made visible with photographic emulsions or by means of cloud chambers, bubble chambers or spark chambers. Each of these pieces of equipment puts to use the ionizing effect of charged particles.

In a cloud chamber, for instance, the volume of the container is rapidly expanded in order to produce a rapid cooling of the gas, thereby raising its humidity above 100 percent. When a charged particle passes through the chamber, droplets form around the ions it produces. As a result, its trail can be detected and photographed.

A bubble chamber is similar to a cloud chamber, but uses a liquid, which is maintained almost at its boiling point. The pressure is suddenly reduced so that the temperature of the liquid is above its boiling point for that pressure, but the timing of the pressure drop is such that boiling begins only on ions left by particles passing through at that moment. At the same time the chamber is illuminated so that the trails of bubbles can be photographed. Because a liquid is many times as dense as a gas, a bubble chamber can record more events than a cloud chamber of the same size. Liquid hydrogen, deuterium, he-

A spark chamber

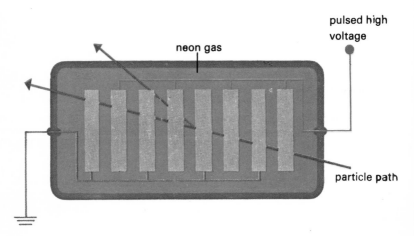

lium, propane and a number of other liquids have been utilized in bubble chambers.

In a spark chamber a number of metal plates are placed a few millimeters apart and surrounded by an inert atmosphere. The voltage of every other plate is raised, perhaps to as much as 30,000 volts. This can be done at the command of a set of instruments, to make the equipment selective for the particles or events being studied. Any ion trail between the plates will cause sparks to jump from plate to plate, and cameras looking between the plates can photograph them.

With the enormous range of powerful accelerators, storage rings and sensitive detectors that have become available to the nuclear physicist, the progress in understanding the microstructure of matter has been rapid. Already well over a hundred particles have been identified, although it may turn out that some of these are excited states of others. The giant proton synchrotrons and other advanced machines will continue the progress toward determining what really are the basic units of matter.

A cloud chamber

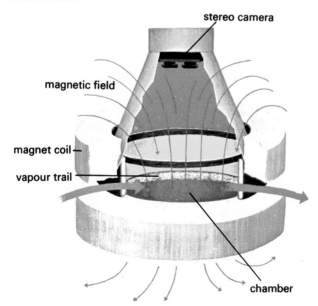

stereo camera

magnetic field

magnet coil

vapour trail

chamber

Bubble chamber photographs look like this. This one shows that a high-energy X-ray changed its mass and energy into an electron and a positron. These move in spirals because of the magnetic field of the chamber.

In this reaction an antiproton collided with an ordinary proton. Both were completely annihilated, their mass and kinetic energy changing into mesons which then changed into other lighter particles.

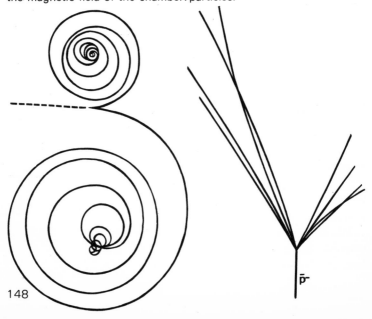

$\bar{p}^-$

PEACEFUL USES OF NUCLEAR EXPLOSIONS

On December 10, 1967, nuclear explosive equivalent to about 20,000 tons of TNT was detonated about four-fifths of a mile below the ground in New Mexico; the aim was to free the rich reserves of natural gas believed to be trapped tightly in the sandstone at this level. Called the Gasbuggy Project, it was the first real application of explosives in the American Project Plowshare, which aims to learn how to apply nuclear energy to specific uses, safely, economically and with precision. Previous explosions had been intended to provide a clearer understanding of crater and cavity formation, and to obtain data on the effects of explosions on different types of rock; obviously much had also been learned from the weapons testing program, and Plowshare scientists now have the experience of well over two hundred nuclear explosions.

In a nuclear explosion the energy is released in less than one-millionth of a second. It is in three forms: kinetic energy, thermal radiation and nuclear radiation (neutron and gamma rays). Material near the center of a nuclear explosion is heated to tens of millions of degrees, and the bubble of gas expands rapidly; much of its energy is transferred to the surroundings as a strong shock wave, moving outward. This, in an underground explosion, melts, cracks and crushes the surrounding rock.

The depth at which the explosion occurs, together with the physical properties of the surrounding rock, determine whether a cavity or a crater will be formed; it also decides the size of the crater. In cavity formation, when cavity growth stops, broken rock may fall from the ceiling and the walls, resulting in the formation of a crudely hemispheric room; generally the entire cavity roof falls in, and rock above it, fractured by the shock wave, does likewise, producing a tall chimney several times the volume of the original cavity. It is almost filled with broken, highly permeable material, usually with a small cavity at the top.

With thermonuclear explosions it is at least technically possible to carry out a number of operations, safely and, because thermonuclear explosion gives the cheapest 'big

Nevada Test Site: Crater was formed by the explosion of a thermonuclear device of about 100 kilotons on July 6, 1962 in the
desert alluvial soil as part of the United States Atomic Energy
Commission's 'Project Plowshare'. This experiment, known as
Project Sedan, left a crater of 1,200 feet in diameter and 320
feet in depth. About 7.5 million cubic feet of earth were removed
by this explosion. The buried charge that produced this crater was
about five times more powerful than the bomb dropped on Hiroshima in 1945.

150

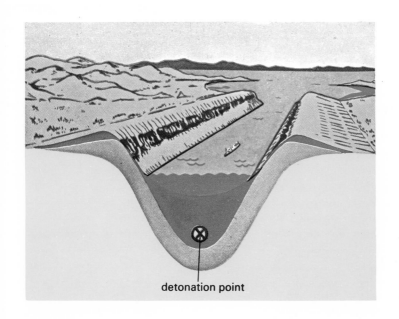

detonation point

A sea-level canal could be dug by nuclear explosives.

bang', economically. One of the great visions of the program is a sea-level 'Panama' canal, which could be produced by a series of explosions. A number of sites in Central America have been examined, and in each case the cost would be much lower with thermonuclear explosive. Furthermore, the canal could be 1,000 feet wide and 60 feet deep. Nuclear explosions could also be used to break up ore bodies for mining. The ore could then be recovered from the cavity by standard mining techniques, or by pumping in acid to dissolve the metal and then pumping the solution to the surface. New harbors could be dug, and this would allow ships to be built deeper, and canyon walls could be collapsed to form dams. In addition, new elements can be created by exposing targets made from heavy elements to the intense neutron flux produced by a thermonuclear explosion.

Indeed, although there will always be political, social and safety limitations to the use of thermonuclear explosions, the future is nevertheless an exciting one.

Hungarian researchers measure the amount of radioactive fertilizer used by rice plants.

INTERNATIONAL ORGANIZATIONS

Research into and the development of the many peaceful uses of atomic energy are costly and may absorb a comparatively large part of a country's resources. As a result, several international organizations have come into existence to promote and direct collaboration between nations.

The *International Atomic Energy Agency* (IAEA) was set up in 1957 under the auspices of the United Nations. More than ninety nations are members, and they include all the countries with advanced knowledge of atomic energy. The agency helps to disseminate technical experience and knowledge among its members and to set up international standards. It publishes scientific reports and organizes international meetings. In the field of nuclear power, the IAEA has helped to establish international safety codes and guarantees that power reactors are not used for military purposes. In agriculture, the IAEA has sponsored research projects into fertilizers and pest control using radioisotopes. Radioisotopes are also being used under IAEA direction for medical diagnosis and treatment in developing countries. The agency has its headquarters in Vienna, Austria and maintains several laboratories and research stations in other countries.

Three important organizations exist in Europe. The

European Nuclear Energy Agency (ENEA) consists of eighteen European countries with the United States and Canada as associate members. It was formed in 1957. It has the same general purposes as the IAEA but is concerned only with western Europe. The ENEA also acts as a coordinating body for the development of atomic energy to meet future European energy needs. The *European Atomic Energy Community* (Euratom) again has the same general purposes as the other agencies; it was formed in 1958. Its membership is limited to the countries of the European Economic Community (the Common Market). The headquarters are at Brussels, Belgium.

International cooperation among European countries in nuclear physics takes place at the laboratories of the *European Organization for Nuclear Research* (CERN) near Geneva, Switzerland. CERN operates one of the largest particle accelerators in the world and has been responsible for several advances in fundamental nuclear physics.

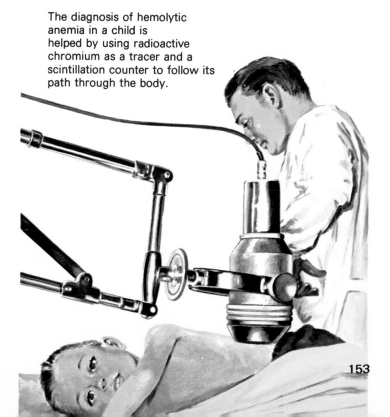

The diagnosis of hemolytic anemia in a child is helped by using radioactive chromium as a tracer and a scintillation counter to follow its path through the body.

KEY EVENTS IN THE HISTORY OF THE ATOM

1803 Dalton established the theory that matter consists of atoms.

1895 Röntgen discovers X-rays

1896 Radioactivity discovered by Becquerel.

1897 Electron named by Thomson.

1898 Radium isolated by Pierre and Marie Curie.

1902 Rutherford and Soddy explain radioactive decay —elements change into other elements releasing energy in the process.

1905 Einstein published his Theory of Special Relativity and showed that mass is equivalent to energy ($E = mc^2$).

1910 Soddy showed existence of isotopes—forms of elements with same chemical properties but different atomic weights.

1911 Rutherford showed that the positive charge of an atom is concentrated in a heavy 'nucleus'.

1919 Rutherford achieved the first artificial nuclear transmutation by disintegrating nitrogen into oxygen and hydrogen through the use of alpha particles.

1928 Separately Condon and Gurney and Gamow explained how alpha particles are emitted from the nucleus.

1931 Deuterium, later to be used in the first H-bomb, discovered by Urey.

1932 Chadwick discovered the neutron. Cockroft and Walton artificially disintegrated nuclei— first experimental verification of Einstein's equation ($E = mc^2$).

1938 Fission discovered by Hahn and Strassman; explained by Meitner and Frisch.

1940 Seaborg and McMillan discover plutonium, a satisfactory substitute for rare U-235.

1942 Fermi built and operated the first nuclear reactor.

1945 First nuclear explosion took place at Alamogordo, New Mexico on 7/16; first used at Hiroshima on 8/6.

1952 The U.S. tested H-bomb in the Pacific on 11/1.

1954 *U.S.S. Nautilus* launched, first atomic submarine.

1956 First atomic reactor to produce electricity opened at Calder Hall, England.

1957 Shippingport reactor, first U.S. atomic electrical reactor begins operating.

1959 Dounreay fast reactor commissioned.

1961 Radioisotope-powered electric power generator placed in orbit; first use of nuclear power in space.

1961 U.S. begins Project Ploughshare, nuclear explosions for peaceful purposes.

1962 *U.S. Nuclear Ship Savannah* launched, first atomic powered ship.

1965 First nuclear reactor (SNAP 10A) operated in space.

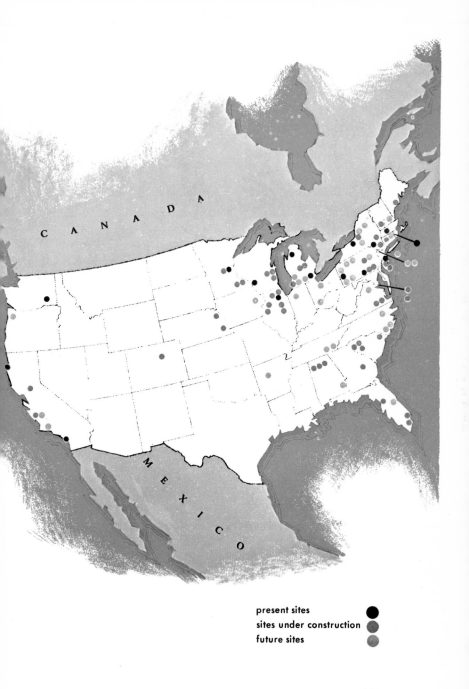

present sites ●
sites under construction ●
future sites ●

155

BOOKS TO READ

The World of the Atom. Henry A. Boorse and Lloyd Motz (eds.) (2 vols.). Basic Books, 1966. Original scientific papers by the great discovery-makers of atomic science, with historical commentary by the editors.

Roads to Discovery. Ralph Lapp. Harper & Row, 1960.

Men and Atoms. William L. Laurence. Simon & Schuster, 1959.

Inside the Atom. Issac Asimov. 3rd revised edition. Abelard Schuman, 1966.

Manhattan Project. S. Groueff. Little, Brown, 1967.

The Atom. Charles Hatcher. Macmillan, 1963.

Atoms for Peace. David Oakes Woodbury. 2nd revised edition. Dodd, Mead, 1965.

Atoms for the World. Laura Fermi. University of Chicago Press, 1957.

Peacetime Uses of Atomic Energy. Martin Mann. Viking, 1961.

Atomic Submarines. Norman Polmar. Van Nostrand, 1963.

Kill and Overkill. Ralph Lapp. Basic Books, 1962.

The Legacy of Hiroshima. Edward Teller. Doubleday, 1962.

INDEX

DATE DUE

JAN 5 1979			
APR 1 9 1980			
MAY 1 8 1980			
MAR 2 1981			
MAY 2 1 1981			
FEB 04 1982			
APR 23 1984			
APR 2 3 1986			
APR 2 2 1987			
DEC 1 1 1987			
APR 2 6 1989			
GAYLORD			PRINTED IN U.S.A.